D0151420

WOMEN
AND
SACRIFICE

WOMEN AND SACRIFICE

MALE NARCISSISM AND THE PSYCHOLOGY OF RELIGION

William Beers

 Wayne State University Press   Detroit

Library of Congress Cataloging-in-Publication Data

Beers, William, 1948–
    Women and sacrifice : male narcissism and the psychology of
religion / William Beers.
      p.   cm.
    Includes bibliographical references and index.
    ISBN 0-8143-2377-4 (alk. paper)
    1. Sacrifice—Psychology.   2. Violence—Religious aspects—
Psychology.   3. Narcissism—Religious aspects.   4. Sexism in
religion.   5. Lord's Supper—Episcopal Church—Psychology.
6. Sacrifice—Vanuatu—Malekula—Psychology. I. Title.
BL570.B43 1992
291.3′4′019—dc20   92-13007

Designer: Mary Krzewinski

Cover art: Mary Krzewinski

To
BREN AND CAM
AND TO
JIM, LIDDY, AND JOHN

Destiny. My destiny! Droll thing life is—that mysterious arrangement of merciless logic for a futile purpose. The most you can hope for is some knowledge of yourself that comes too late—a crop of unextinguishable regrets. I have wrestled with death. It is the most unexciting contest you can imagine. It takes place in an impalpable grayness, with nothing underfoot, with nothing around, without spectators, without clamor, without glory, without the great desire for victory, without the great fear of defeat, in a sickly atmosphere of tepid skepticism, without much belief in yourself and still less in that of your adversary. If such is the form of ultimate wisdom, then life is a greater mystery than some of us think it to be.

Joseph Conrad, *Heart of Darkness*

CONTENTS

1

PART TWO
The Dynamic Psychology of Sacrifice, Symbol, and Dread

PART THREE
Narcissism, Women, and Sacrifice

PREFACE

JOSEPH CONRAD'S BOOKS, particularly his *Heart of Darkness*, have influenced the way I have understood life and the focus of my work. His fundamental questions about human feeling and motivation— the maddening search for the dark reasons why men do what they do in their horror, despair, loneliness, rage, and lust—helped shape this account I have written about men, women, and sacrifice. But there have been others who have more significantly influenced my reckoning with human horror. John Loose, professor of religion and literature at Gettysburg College, profoundly affected my initial descent into horror. He called the experience the "ecstasy of horror," but I came to see after his death that this ecstatic experience may have veiled a deeper horror of grief—his alcoholism, cancer, and intellectualism weaving the fabric of an inability to mourn. Perhaps Kafka was right when he wrote that there is "only one illness, and medicine hunts it down blindly like a beast through unending forests." John Loose's illness—the illness of most men—is the inability to mourn.

I am also thankful to Leighton McCutchen, visiting lecturer at Harvard University, who first introduced me to disease and grief in the works of Freud, David Bakan, and Gotthard Booth, and who helped me see both in myself. Finally, Peter Homans, with whom I studied the psychology of religion at the University of Chicago, continues to help in my effort to understand and appropriate mourning as an existential prerequisite for creation and growth. Gratitude to

5

these men notwithstanding, this effort to express an en-gendered view of men, religion, and culture is mine, however, and not mere filial piety echoing any previous teacher's work.

As I began this study of sacrifice, my companion, Janet Hollis Beers, was a counselor at an Evanston, Illinois, shelter for battered women. As I sought the archaic history and psychology of sacrifice and as Janet witnessed the effects of male violence against women in modern American society, we realized we were confronting the same reality. I am grateful for and a bit envious of Janet's courage and patience in our life together for over twenty years.

Finally, I express my appreciation to Jean Comaroff, Joan Hemenway, Elaine Koza, Susan Henking, Mary Ellen Ross, and Kelley Raab for commenting on chapters and earlier versions of this work.

Books, wrote Conrad, "share with us the great incertitude of ignominy or glory—of severe justice and senseless persecution—of calumny and misunderstanding—the shame of undeserved glory." Books "contain our very thought, our ambitions, our indignations, our illusions, our fidelity to truth, our persistent leaning towards error." Some books—I suspect including this one—are efforts to resolve conflicts we may be too unsure of or too late to address directly to those who, in the midst of idealized transference and countertransference, paradoxically excited and delayed us. What is so wonderful about psychology is that since we use it to explain the behavior of others, we are required to be honest about its use on our own behavior as well. When I first read *Heart of Darkness*, the horror that Kurtz knew all too well connected with my own horror—partially concealed behind my adolescent fortress of rebellion, desire, and despair. During the ensuing quarter century, I sought out horror—not the media horror of popular culture but the horror of an inescapable recognition.

On my first night as a chaplain in an inner city hospital, I walked into the trauma room seeking information for a family anxiously sitting in what the emergency department staff referred to as the "grieving room." As I pushed through the door, the resident had his bloodied hand plunged into the chest of the victim, massaging his heart. Yet that was not the face of horror. The real horror was in the eyes of the woman who was told ten minutes later that the baby she had once pushed out from between her legs and who had sucked milk from her body was now a dead man. ("Mistah Kurtz—he dead.") Or the horror of the seventy-five-year-old grieving widow who told me that her heart would pound with desire and fear as she sat in church looking at the near-naked body of Christ being tortured on the cross.

My examples of women's horror in the face of men's violence are not accidental. But while women's horror is real, it is the horror within *men's* experience, particularly as it is embodied in ritual violence, that I address in this book. Women have been proceeding rather nicely with the development of their own psychology. Less lyrical and more demythologized than Robert Bly's *Iron John*, this book is a contribution to an important aspect of men's psychology. I have sought to understand the psychological meaning and function of sacrifice by working within existing scholarly disciplines. I do feel, nevertheless, a bit like the character Marlow in *Heart of Darkness*, for it has seemed at times that I, too, am trying to describe a dream, even a nightmare. And there is something nightmarish about the psychological study of religious man. Often his loftiest intentions conceal the darkest, dreadful longings of his heart. In this book I claim that his most sacred of rituals remains his most narcissistic and violent. I argue that the Christian eucharist has a psychological function that diminishes and controls women. I insist that men so fear women that their religious rituals often exclude women in order to gain power over them. These are hard things to say, particularly to religious men. Trying to convince readers of this is perhaps not unlike Marlow trying to convince his listeners that a man such as Kurtz actually existed, that such men as *we* know these horrors as well. But that is my task.

Introduction

Do you see him? Do you see the story? Do you see anything? It seems to me I am trying to tell you a dream—making a vain attempt, because no relation of a dream can convey the dream-sensation, that commingling of absurdity, surprise, and bewilderment in a tremor of struggling revolt, that notion of being captured by the incredible which is the very essence of dreams.

Joseph Conrad, *Heart of Darkness*

THE QUESTION

THIS BOOK HAS two related purposes. First, it serves as a psychocultural introduction to ritual blood sacrifice. The term *psychocultural* does not imply an intellectual hybridization, such as "psychoanalytic sociology." Rather, it inscribes an interdisciplinary process that leaves anthropology, sociology, and psychoanalytic psychology as distinct yet complementary disciplines. The premise for including the three disciplines is that their combination can reveal most profoundly the subtle and horrific fabric of sacrifice. Each chapter introduces an orientation that illuminates particular aspects of the psychocultural phenomenon of sacrifice.

Second, this book is a psychoanalytic essay about sacrifice. This second purpose is really the engine that has driven the whole project. Alfred North Whitehead spoke of two types of experience. One type is consciously accessible and repeatable, the experience of the everyday world in which we live. "The other type," continued Whitehead, "is vague, haunting, unmanageable . . . heavy with the contact of things gone by, which lay their grip on our immediate selves" (1927, 43–44), what Joseph Conrad termed the "essence of dreams." Psychoanalysis concerns itself with this second type, which beats in the more private, internal hearts of men and lies partially concealed in religious sacrifice—the ritual act of killing something for sacred purposes. This book, then, is a psychological journey into the vague, haunting, and unmanageable internal life of man the sacrificer.

Of necessity, that journey has taken me into the work of anthropologists and sociologists. I have maintained an appreciation for both disciplines, and while my conclusions may be considered more strictly psychological, they do not contradict anthropological or sociological evidence. In fact, I believe the theory I propose in this book complements anthropological theories of sacrifice. I also believe it completes earlier dynamic psychological theories of sacrifice, which have been unacceptable to anthropology.

Blood sacrifice is a highly evocative ritual experience; it is an equally evocative subject to study. Who does not squirm a bit over images of human or animal sacrifice? A human being is drugged and held over a wedge-shaped monolith while an Aztec priest, using an obsidian knife, slices open the victim's abdomen, just below the rib cage, thrusts his hand into the incision up into the chest cavity, and rips out the still-beating heart. A bleating goat is held to the ground on its back while it is cut completely in two, including the genitals. And then there are the sacrifices of hundreds of screaming pigs of Malekula to be discussed in chapter 11. This sacrifice business is a subject to which we keep returning because it affects us so viscerally, and intellectual rationalization—the so-called logic of sacrifice—never fully satisfies. Like others I too have been lured by the darker existential question of what motivates men to do what they do. Why do they make things bleed and die in the name of the sacred?

As absurd and surprising as the answer to that question might appear, as much as it might offend our religious sensibilities or psychologically wound our narcissism, I have been encouraged by men and women who have also glimpsed facets of the psychological reality I am proposing. David Bakan's book, *Disease, Pain, and Sacrifice*, is intended to be about the psychology of suffering. But his conclusions are applicable to the study of ritual sacrifice. First, he writes that "there is an intrinsic relationship among separation-estrangement, physical disease, and the psychological condition associated with sacrifice" (Bakan 1968, 99). Separation or estrangement from meaningful social context greatly increases the risk of physical disease. In illness, the ego defends against disease through organic isolation (e.g., in the form of a simple infection, a tumor, or the involvement of an organ or organ system). Bakan understands that the ego's isolation of disease is a kind of sacrifice. "Our thought is brought to the idea of sacrifice in which that which is 'me' is made into something which is 'not-me,' and in which that 'not-me' is sacrificed in order that 'I' might continue to live" (79).

Bakan continues his analysis of disease and sacrifice through a fascinating psychological interpretation of the biblical book of Job. Job's suffering and disease reflect the unconscious projection of a male infanticidal impulse, an impulse that found gruesome expression in ancient eastern Mediterranean cults of child sacrifice. Bakan notes that "the infanticidal impulse in the male is associated, in Western civilization, with patrilineality and the assumption by the male of the responsibility of caring for the children" (104). The suppression of such an impulse (contained in but misrepresented by Freud as the Oedipus complex) is one psychological function of Judaism and Christianity. The psychological rationalization of the repression conceals the shift from the desire for individual survival (in Bakan's view, the original reason for the infanticidal impulse) to the desire for immortality through the survival of one's children. Having children, then, became an important aspect of being a man, and Bakan notes that "there is hardly a page in the Bible on which it is not asserted in one way or another that the male can have children" (119). This desire for immortality, however, may be equivalent to the desire to have children for another psychological reason. In this book I argue that the desire to have children and the desire for immortality are part of a male psychological constellation involving the envy, desire, and fear of women. Nevertheless, one of the burdens of this book is to show that Bakan's statements are profoundly true.

Using current psychoanalytic theory, I explore the psychology of contradiction, gender, and power in male ritual systems of blood sacrifice. This contention—that ritual blood sacrifice is a male or male-identified ritual—is not limited to psychologists such as Bakan. In a recent sociological study of the role of gender in sacrifice, Nancy Jay argues that within patrilineal descent, sacrifice "works as evidence of, and therefore as a means of constituting, lines of patrilineal descent" (1985, 294). The roots and meaning of blood sacrifice, however, are to be found not simply within the patrilineal superstructure of a society. Social order, no matter how much its necessity *appears* to be self-generating and self-perpetuating, is to a significant and radical degree correlated to and motivated by psychological structure. To Jay's sociological assertion, then, I am adding a psychological one:

men seek to control lineal descent out of their own male psychological structure. In sacrifice, the psychological motivation of men is to
control the male-perceived power of women. This is not to say that
the presentation of an explanation of psychological structure—a psychoanalytic explanation—is reductionistic to the detriment of sociocultural explanations. Psychological structures exist in a cultural context that is historically and developmentally necessary and irreducible.
The psychological claims I make are presented in the light of social
structures, cultural expressions, and individual and group history.

ANTHROPOLOGY AND PSYCHOANALYSIS

MANY INFLUENTIAL ANTHROPOLOGISTS have considered psychological issues in their discussions of social behavior and ritual action.
Some have attempted explicit theories of sacrifice, while others have
not. In this book I look at the theories developed by Henri Hubert
and Marcel Mauss, and Claude Lévi-Strauss, theories indebted to Emile
Durkheim. I also review the symbolic anthropology of ritual of Mary
Douglas and Victor Turner, and the cultural anthropology of Clifford Geertz. Each of these reflects on the psychology of ritual, yet,
with the exception of Hubert and Mauss, are less concerned with
sacrifice as a specific object of study. Hubert and Mauss (1964) developed a structural-functional theory of sacrifice. They were influenced by Durkeim, who earlier had argued that the psychology of
religion should confine itself to conscious identification and sentiment, that is, to social representations as expressions of the collective
conscious (Durkheim 1915). The social representations explored were
based predominantly on *male* identifications and sentiment. This makes
their work less helpful in an inclusive theory of religious ritual. But
because this book is about male or male-identified ritual, their work
remains, unintentionally, appropriate. Lévi-Strauss (1966) argued for
a theory of sacrifice based on understanding the "savage mind" within
us all. This "science of the concrete" has many affinities with Jungian
and other post-Freudian psychoanalytic thought.

Douglas (1966, 1975) studied and dismissed Freud in developing her theory of symbol and ritual. She found later object relations theory more helpful in explaining how ritual functions. But she
did not use that same theory to explore the psychology of ritual.
Turner (1978) also encountered Freud. He was impressed by Freud's
"style" of thought, and used such concepts as repression and subli-

mation in a metaphorical sense rather than as psychological explanations. Like Durkheim, Douglas and Turner were concerned more
with social processes than with individual psychodynamics.

Geertz (1973) comes close to recognizing and even naming the
psychological elements to be identified in sacrifice. His work is representative of a number of psychologically oriented anthropologists
who see social conflict (including social transformation) as reflecting
issues of the self and culture rather than as expressions of instinctual,
sexual drives. Unfortunately, Geertz himself never attempted an explicit theory of sacrifice, although I have teased it out of his discussions of religion and culture, in particular that of Balinese cockfights.

Psychoanalysis also has different theoretical orientations. If a
discussion is limited to *explicit* dynamic psychological theories of ritual sacrifice, I could begin with Freud (1913) and the classical drive
theory, and end with Jung and the theory of introversion (1959,
1967). However, just as anthropological theory has changed and re-
fined itself, so too has psychoanalysis. In the course of this book, I
review these explicit psychological theories of sacrifice. Although Freud
and classical theories of sacrifice have, since their inception, been shown
to be woefully inadequate for anthropology, this is not to say that
the theories do not contain useful elements for understanding sacrifice. The same holds true for Jung and analytic psychology.

Although anthropologists have recognized and struggled with
an obvious psychological dimension to ritual behavior, and psychoanalysts have not failed to acknowledge (sometimes a bit grudgingly) the cultural component to psychological apparatus, the relationship between anthropology and psychoanalysis has remained
ambivalent at best. Anthropologists cluster their distrust of psychoanalytic thought around two complaints: ethnocentrism and reductionism. The complainers of ethnocentrism argue that psychoanalysis at best reveals the psychology of the Western mind. In response
to this charge, the anthropologist Obeyesekere (1990) argues that
the bifurcation of mind and culture into Western and non-Western
is a continuation of the same arrogance that gave rise to the former
ethnocentrism of colonial-period anthropologists. In other words, the
retreat into relativism ostensibly to protect the uniqueness of non-
Western cultures belies a deeper arrogance about our Western world.
Challenges to our cultural specialness, then, are much like earlier
challenges to our cosmic, biological, and psychological specialness
(Freud's three narcissistic wounds). Putting it more humorously, Ob-

eyesekere writes: "The Sinhalas have a proverb to describe people in their own society who think they are special. They say 'Have you emerged from an elephant's arse hole?'—as against ordinary people born from human wombs. It is the fact that we are born from human wombs, they say, that gives us our common humanity underlying formal differences. I think psychoanalysis gives us a similar message: Victorian neurotics did not come from an elephant's arse hole, but share instead a common humanity" (218).

Anthropologists have also complained that psychoanalysis "reduces" personal, religious, or cultural phenomena to psychological dynamics or causes and thereby somehow misses their essence. To this complaint Obeyesekere replies that anthropology does a similar thing: "Ethnographic translation is a mode of appropriation of the culture, but not through the fusion of horizons; it incorporates the description of the other into the familiar grammatical and semantic categories of one's own language. This is of course over and above the fact that it is simply impossible for anywhere to present a native point of view since such a viewpoint does not exist" (219). I find Obeyesekere's position appropriate and in no need of lengthy discussion. However, some previous anthropologists read Freud on religion and culture, and then wrote about psychoanalytic theory, forgetting, I suppose, that psychoanalysis itself has a sociology and history not limited to its founder. This is much less the case today (for example, see Herdt's excellent intoduction in Herdt and Stephen 1989). Because this book seeks to understand psychoanalytically the psychology of sacrifice, I take very seriously the historical development of psychoanalysis. For example, while I agree with his arguments about ethnocentrism and reductionism, I do not agree with Obeyesekere's (1990) oedipal interpretation of South Indian myths. In a recent work, De Vos and Suarez-Orozco (1987) discuss earlier preoedipal, oral themes in sacrifice. Unfortunately they avoid drawing conclusions about gender, even though the ethnographic example of the Hauka dog sacrifice is essentially a story about men.

For their part, psychoanalysts have shown little interest in the psychology of sacrifice. This is perhaps a reflection of their reluctance or methodological inability to develop a psychoanalytic theory of culture. Two theoretical schools, however, have affected the orientation of psychoanalysis to a degree that Freud and the first generation of psychoanalysts only dimly perceived: the British school of object relations, informed by analysts such as Melanie Klein, Marion Milner, and D. W. Winnicott, and the American (Chicago) school of self-psychology, initiated by Heinz Kohut. My purpose in presenting several aspects of object relations theory is to indicate how the theory of symbol formation has changed from Freud's original ideas to the theory of narcissism articulated by Kohut. My contention is that Kohut's theory of narcissism can help analyze and explain the psychological structures of sacrifice (including its symbols); and it can, with a careful reading of the clinical material presented by Kohut and self-psychological analysts, account for the gender-specific qualities of male narcissism and of male ritual sacrifice.

There are several areas of mutual concern where dynamic psychology and anthropology converge. The two most obvious are those of the self and symbolization. Both anthropology and psychology want to know the relation between the self, the symbol, and culture. They want to know how one thing comes to stand for something else. Related to the symbol is the concept of classification. How and why do things and ideas become related? Another area of mutual concern is that of change—transition, transformation, separation, dissolution, differentiation—as it relates to individual and social life—birth, growth, death. And lastly, there is mutual interest in the human feeling of anxiety—both individual dread and social tension. Anxiety is the precursor of a whole range of human affect: love, hate, anger, fear, joy, despair, and even peace. It is perhaps the theory of anxiety that has undergone the most significant alterations in the history of dynamic psychology and that is most in need of being reintroduced to anthropology.

The relation between individual anxiety and social tension introduces a key discussion within contemporary anthropology. Although more crudely seen as the dialectic between the individual and society, I understand the debate as one between actual, individual human beings with developmental minds and the society (social structure and culture), or the self and culture (both material and nonmaterial). The problem for sociologists (e.g., Durkheim 1915; Berger and Luckmann 1967) and anthropologists (e.g., Strathern 1988; Comaroff 1985) is that, in an effort to understand the manifest significance and latent ideology of social events, artifacts, or images (culture), they usually neglect to show how this occurs for individual participants. Yet culture is more than its artifacts. Meaning does not reside in the artifact, gesture, or symbol. Even the "agreement" *between* people as to meaning and value does not reside between people but within individual people (where, as object relations has argued, a "between" or transitional space *is* experienced and used).

Of course, with the introduction of psychology, transitional space, and the individual self, some anthropologists might respond with the complaint that both psychology and the "self" are Western bourgeois concepts, which reduce the non-Western to Western categories. I have retold Obeyesekere's response earlier, so the complaint may be true but irrelevant. Yet I still find the anthropological approach a fine fit for the way I have looked at the social world in this book, and I attempt to peer into the social artifact or the gesture and discover the residues of the individual human minds that created them. I am trying to do what William James (1958) avoided in his 1901–1902 lectures on religion. In those lectures James focused on the individual, private religious believer and avoided the institutional, public aspects of religion. I am trying to sense the personal origins and psychodynamics embodied, legitimated, or concealed within the seemingly endless public rituals of sacrifice.

SELF-PSYCHOLOGY AND SACRIFICE

I SHALL BE arguing that sacrifice embodies and conceals the psychological structure of a male anxiety associated with differentiation, separation, and other related transitions. This male anxiety is not the drive anxiety of classical psychoanalytic theory, nor is it the adaptive anxiety of ego psychology, nor the transitional anxiety of object relations theory. Each of these theories may be useful in indicating an aspect of anxiety evident in the psychological structure of sacrifice. With Kohut's self-psychology and his theory of narcissism, however, we have a mode of analysis and explanation that takes into account the varying objects and relations of sacrifice and does not conflict with symbolic or cultural anthropological theory in the way Freudian thought does. An understanding of narcissistic anxiety is the key to understanding the psychological structure of sacrifice.

Classical psychoanalytic theory maintains one type of anxiety: separation or oedipal anxiety. Kohut, in perhaps his most radical departure from classical theory, argues for a second type: disintegration anxiety. "The core of disintegration anxiety is the anticipation of the breakup of the self, not the fear of the drive" (1978, 104). He further states that the intensity of drives is not the cause of psychopathology, but a result of it. In the clinical practice of psychoanalysis, there may be difficulty in distinguishing between the two types of anxiety because disintegration anxiety is often verbalized by the analysand as separation anxiety. Kohut's most significant clinical contribution is his further refinement of the theory and practice of empathic introspection as the means of distinguishing between the two types of anxiety. He initially placed self-dissolution anxiety prior to separation-drive anxiety, but in the end even believed that so-called oedipal anxiety grew out of unincorporated narcissism, and not out of unresolved drive issues.

Kohut was interested in both the use and influence of psychoanalytic theory. He wrote extensively on the psychoanalytic interpretation of art and history, seeing in psychoanalysis a crucial asset in the development of a theory of culture. His remarks on religion are limited and unsystematic. There is every indication, however, that had he lived a bit longer he might well have expanded his understanding of such concepts as *cosmic narcissism*, and other terms. I can find in his work no interest in religious rituals or in the methodological relationship with anthropology. Nevertheless, I contend that Kohut's development of self-psychology and the theory of narcissism is profound not only in it clinical contributions, but in its usefulness as a means of delineating and explaining the psychological structure of ritual sacrifice. In a self-psychological understanding of ritual, blood sacrifice functions to reduce the self's experience of overstimulating idealizations or shameful grandiosity, a result of anxiety associated with differentiation, separation, and dissolution anxiety. This anxiety reflects esteem and identification issues rather than drive issues. Moreover, after a close examination of Kohut's and other self-psychologists' clinical material, the anxiety reveals itself to be male in both its psychological structure and its sociocultural manifestations.

FEMINIST THEORY AND THE SOCIAL SCIENCES

MY ASSERTION THAT the anxiety contained within the psychological structure of sacrifice is male begs another question: What about women? This question refers to women in two contexts: the cultural context of ritual sacrifice and the context of social scientific theory—anthropology and psychoanalysis. Many women (and increasingly more men) social scientists have made the unassailable claim that women and the social context of women have not been studied in the same way men have been studied. As two women anthropologists have

written, with some exceptions (most of them women), "anthropologists in writing about human culture have followed our own culture's ideological bias in treating women as relatively invisible and
describing what are largely the activities and interests of men" (Rosaldo and Lamphere 1974, 2). They contend that this "ideological
bias" is worth examining from both contextual points of view (cultural and methodological) because they are in fact identical; that is,
the methodological bias *is* a cultural bias.

When this bias is taken seriously and the cultural roles and
meanings of and for women are examined, anthropologists have discovered that the cultural asymmetry of men and women reflects an
underlying subordination of women to men. As social subordination
and its cultural structures and symbols (including rituals) are evident
to enlightened anthropology, efforts to explain how it is that women
are culturally subordinate to men reveal a deep, powerful, and culturally pervasive male anxiety about women. Summarizing one article
on work and sex in a Guatemalan village, Rosaldo and Lamphere
note: "[Village women's] ideas about the body have two aspects: in
work the body is competent and skillful; in sex and reproduction it
is changeable, mysterious, and a source of danger. Sex, then, provides
a cultural rationale for female subordination; at the same time, the
very mystery of a woman's body unites her to conceptions of the
cosmos, and powers that may be threatening to men" (13).

If feminist anthropology recognizes a relation between a perception of female power and its presumed threat to men, it tends to
explain the cultural results of such a relation by staying within the
familiar anthropological (Marxist) areas of consciousness (and false
consciousness), ideology, symbolic structure and classification, and
social contradiction. Such anthropology seems more concerned with
righting a cultural and intellectual wrong by presenting the neglected
female side of human culture. These efforts extend to the area of the
psychological anthropology of feminine personality (Chodorow 1974).
But such efforts are not primarily concerned with explaining why the
male perception of female power is accompanied by anxiety—the experience (at a deep, even unconscious level) of women as dangerous
and threatening. Moreover, such efforts remain cultural in their orientation, that is, gender personality is seen as a culturation process:
men fear women because they are brought up to do so. In this book
I shall argue that the culturation of male attitudes and beliefs about
women is a secondary process that fuels and responds to a more

primitive psychological experience, which Kohut's theory of narcissism helps us understand.

In a like fashion, feminist critiques have also made their way into psychoanalytic theory. Besides well-worn criticisms of classical psychoanalytic theory, there is a significant gender question raised about the very theory I shall be using in this book (Philipson 1985). The central question is: Whose narcissism? If blood sacrifice is a gender-specific and male-identified rite, and if, as I argue, that rite expresses male narcissistic anxiety, then Kohut's theory of narcissism will need a clarifying revision—something I have alluded to several times in this introduction. That revision stems from a review of the clinical examples of self-psychological psychoanalysis presented by Kohut and other psychoanalysts.

METHOD AND THEORY APPLIED: SACRIFICE REVISITED

THIS BOOK IS about a theory of analysis and explanation. It is also about the application of that theory to two distinct ritual sacrificial systems. The sacrificial system of Malekula (Melanesia) represents a non-Western ritual that underwent severe changes from the time it was first studied and recorded by Western anthropologists. Elements of human sacrifice, cannibalism, patrilineal descent, gender issues, and Western effects on the culture are known from the studies of John Layard and others done before the 1920s (Layard 1942; Harrison 1939). Layard has a keen awareness of Jung's archetypal psychology, which guides him not only in what he looks at but in what he writes down, particularly in the area of interpretation of symbols and their psychological explanation. His Jungian orientation, while cumbersome, is fortuitous for us because Jung's metapsychological theory, when it is structurally tamed, has affinities with Kohut's theory, which should not be lost in the extreme debate between classical and Jungian theory.

The second sacrificial complex is the beliefs and practices of the Christian eucharist, in particular, the rites as they appear in *The Book of Common Prayer* (1977) of the Episcopal church in America. Using Kohut's theory of narcissism, I argue that the male narcissistic anxiety, which anthropology and psychology find operating in the Malekula example, is no less present in a late twentieth-century American culture.

I have divided this book into three parts comprised of short chapters. In Part I, I present a review of anthropological theories of ritual and sacrifice, including Hubert, Mauss, and Durkheim, Lévi-Strauss, Douglas and Turner, Geertz, and Jay. Part II contains a review of dynamic psychological theories of ritual and symbol, and a review of recent psychoanalytic theories of sacrifice proposed by René Girard and Eli Sagan. Part III includes chapters on Kohut's theory of narcissism, the use of that theory in a social scientific theory of sacrifice, and chapters on Malekulan and Episcopal ritual. Finally in the Conclusion, I suggest how helpful self-psychology is in the specific area of a psychoanalytic theory of religion and the more general problem of a theory of culture.

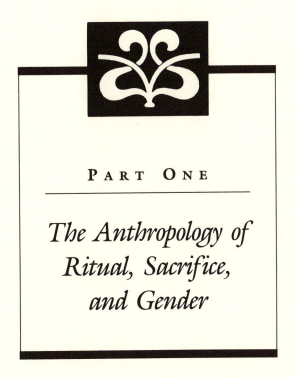

PART ONE

The Anthropology of
Ritual, Sacrifice,
and Gender

ONE

Hubert, Mauss, and Durkheim: The Role of Sentiment, Classification, and Moral Exchange in Ritual and Sacrifice

We penetrated deeper and deeper into the heart of darkness. . . . We were wanderers on a prehistoric earth, on an earth that wore the aspect of an unknown planet. We could have fancied ourselves the first of men taking possession of an accursed inheritance, to be subdued at the cost of profound anguish and of excessive toil. . . .

The earth seemed unearthly. We are accustomed to look upon the shackled form of a conquered monster, but there—there you could look at a thing monstrous and free. It was unearthly, and the men were— No, they were not inhuman. Well, you know, that was the worst of it—this suspicion of their not being inhuman. It would come slowly to one. They howled and leaped, and spun, and made horrid faces; but what thrilled you was just the thought of their humanity— like yours—the thought of your remotest kinship with this wild and passionate uproar.

Joseph Conrad, *Heart of Darkness*

THE HUMAN ACTIVITY of culture, including religious rituals of blood sacrifice, contains expressions of moods and motivations (Geertz 1973). Some motivations are deeper, more hidden than others. Although the specific symbolic activity is artifactual, its deeper motivations are

23

psychical. This psychological dimension cannot be ignored by the social scientist. Yet contemporary anthropologists, as Obeyesekere notes, "make a parallel distinction between mind and culture, motivation and symbolic forms, even though they are willing to recognize that culture is generated out of the mind of people" (1990, 285). The web of oppression, for example, is not merely woven by ideology and tradition. Patriarchy does not exist simply because of man's social and logical systems. These social structures and the cultures they contain are woven by actual, living weavers. Blood sacrifice reflects something deep within men's psyches—be they memories, dreams, fantasies, ideals, and feelings (conscious or unconscious)— and anyone seeking to explain human thought and action would be hard pressed to avoid the realization that there is something psychologically internal to cultural thought and action. An anthropologist who ignores the culturally expressed psychological experiences of anger, hatred, fear, love, or ecstasy is, I think, being dishonest not only with the subject but perhaps even with herself or himself as well. By saying that, however, I am not suggesting a facile oversimplification of the problem for psychoanalytic explanations of sacrifice. The German historian Burkert risks as much when he asserts (without, I think, an adequate psychological context) that "ritual [such as sacrifice] emphasizes and guides individual phantasies" (1972, 75). The specific purpose of a survey of anthropology, then, is to acquire the psychological questions from the anthropologists themselves. My survey of anthropological descriptions and interpretations focuses on those with at least some recognition of the problem of psychology and ritual, if not some acknowledgement, however grudgingly, of something psychological within ritual. My aim throughout this book is to develop a theory of blood sacrifice that includes a dynamic psychology. In this chapter I begin with the functional sociological definition of sacrifice proposed by Hubert and Mauss.

HUBERT AND MAUSS: A FUNCTIONAL THEORY OF SACRIFICE

BECAUSE IT IS the central act of many religions and rituals in all but a small number of cultures, sacrifice has previously received much attention. One of the first and most important interpretations of sacrifice in this century was made by Henri Hubert and Marcel Mauss (1964). Building on the sociological theory of Emile Durkheim, they sought to delineate both the structure and moral function of sacrifice. At the time they wrote their theory, there were three main anthropological theories proposed.

In the late nineteenth century, Edward B. Tylor (1871, 1878) had proposed his theory of sacrifice as gift. This was followed by W. Robertson Smith's (1894) theory of sacrifice as a totemic communal meal. The last major theory of sacrifice proposed by the turn of the century was James Frazer's (1910, 1922) theory of expiation. All of these were criticized by Hubert and Mauss because each theory sought to explain the great variety of sacrificial forms through the use of too arbitrary a principle. Hubert and Mauss were particularly critical of the theory of totemism. Freud had referred to both Robertson Smith and Frazer in his effort to provide anthropological credence for his oedipal psychology. But even Freud realized that the theory of totemism was highly problematic. Totemism is so rare that to make it the basis for interpreting so widespread a phenomenon as sacrifice is perhaps pointless.

Hubert and Mauss understood sacrifice as "a religious act which, through the consecration of a victim, modifies the condition of a moral person who accomplishes it or that of certain objects with which he is concerned" (13). According to this understanding, the consecrated victim serves the purpose of an intermediary between the sacrificer (the person or the object to be beneficially and morally modified by the sacrifice) and the divinity to whom the sacrifice is directed. That which is human and that which is divine are not in direct contact, but are united symbolically or connected in some way through the immolation of the intermediary victim. The reason for the sacrifice in the first place, despite the variety of occasions and specific intended purposes, has to do with a perceived threat to a *moral* order. The sacrifice acknowledges, strengthens, maintains, and/or restores a divine moral order that has been or could be transgressed. The sacrifice involves not only making the victim sacred in the movement from the profane toward the sacred, but the sacrifice modifies the moral condition of the sacrificer or object (e.g., the community, the crops) and restores the divinely ordained order in a movement from the sacred back to the profane.

Hubert and Mauss believed that during particularly serious sacrifices, as when the moral order is upset in such a way as to affect the whole community or when the effects desired are particularly serious, in addition to the three elements of sacrificer, victim, and divinity, an intermediary or guide is mandatory: the "priest." Closer to the sacred, more knowledgeable of the rituals, the priest insures that the beneficial moral modifications desired will not be denied through errors of ritual. On the dynamic relationship between the sacred and the profane, Hubert and Mauss state that "it is . . . a remarkable fact that, in a general way, sacrifice could serve two such contradictory aims as that of inducing a state of sanctity and that of dispelling a state of sin" (58). The victim is made sacred and profane simultaneously at the moment of slaughter. The victim is sacred by virtue of its relation to the divine and profane through its relation to the sacrificer. An ambiguous tension resides within the victim, for at the moment of death the sacred is profaned and the profane made sacred. Thus, in order to understand the function of sacrifice we are compelled to accept a structural ambivalence or paradox.

Hubert and Mauss have presented a very useful understanding of sacrifice. The dynamic relationship between moral order, guilt, victim, sacrificer, and priest seems to represent effectively the ideological meaning of sacrifice. There are, however, several problems with their functionalist interpretation. For some reason they have failed to explain why priest and victim are both intermediaries. If the priest "stands between the sacred and the profane worlds and represents them both" (23), why is the sacrificial procedure—the means of communicating between the sacred and the profane through the mediation of a victim—necessary? Their confusion with the significant elements within the sacrificial system is due in part to an inadequate understanding of the intended function of the sacrificial victim. I am not suggesting that communication does not occur, nor am I denying a theological interpretation. I am questioning the appeal to a paradox to explain why a creature has to bleed and die in order to communicate with the divine or restore moral order. Such an appeal does not answer the question at all. As anthropologists, Hubert and Mauss resort to a theologically circular argument from where they cannot adequately examine the cultural system they wish to understand.

When Hubert and Mauss rejected Frazer's notion of sacrifice as a totemic slaughter and meal, they correctly saw the error of the universal occurrence of the sacrifice and consumption of a god (or totem). By rejecting both Frazer's and Robertson Smith's interpretations, however, they rejected an idea that could clear up some of the confusion in their own theory: the idea of the surrogate or substitute victim. The sacrificial victim is not merely the mediator in the communication between the sacred and the profane. The victim is also not merely the substitute for some (totemic) divinity. The victim is the substitute for the one guilty of transgression, moral confusion, or impurity. Seen in this way, the priest now becomes the mediator and the victim becomes the substitute given to the divinity in the place of the one who has transgressed the moral order. The notion of "priest" does not hold up in a cross-cultural analysis of sacrifice. While some cultures may use a priest or priest-like equivalent, others do not.

In rejecting Tylor's interpretation of sacrifice as a gift, Hubert and Mauss were reacting against a too-generalized application of what appears to be true of only particular sacrifices. Some sacrifices are, however, thought of as gifts. Mauss notes that a very important element of any gift giving is the moral obligation to offer a gift in return (*do ut des*: give and thus receive). There is an obligation to give, an obligation to receive that gift, and an obligation to offer a gift in return. Mauss refers to this as the "contractual sacrifice" (1954, 15). The idea of sacrifice as gift, however, need not contradict the idea of the surrogate (substitute) victim. Sacrifice as gift is equivalent to sacrifice as substitution because the unifying concept in both gift and substitution is that of *exchange*. While the notion of sacrifice as gift does not appear universal, the idea of exchange does. This is why Hubert and Mauss insist that sacrifice intends through exchange to substitute one moral condition for another. For Hubert and Mauss, the necessity for moral exchange exists in the first place because of the existence of moral classifications, which are part of any social group. Moral exchange is in fact social exchange. The exchange of meaning and value through classificatory systems is accomplished by cultural rituals such as sacrifice.

DURKHEIM: SENTIMENT AND CLASSIFICATION

IN ANOTHER BOOK, Mauss and Emile Durkheim ask how it is that people come to classify moral and religious ideas in the way they do. They argue that humans lack the innate propensity to classify (1963, 7). A developing human being needs to be taught to classify. The model containing the categories for classification is society itself. Moreover, moral and religious classification reflects social reality. This idea—that society is the basis for religious and moral categories—was expanded to include all categories of human thought. And Durkheim uses this as the basic thesis of his major work on the origin and meaning of religion (1915).

Social realities, then, for example, families, moieties, or clans, are themselves the bases for what drives men to classify reality in the way that they do. This means that it is not the logic or appearance of logic that fuels the propensity to classify. Rather, it is the way things are experienced affectively as extensions or "representations" of (their affinity with) the social life of a people. For Durkheim and Mauss, *sentiment* is the answer to the question of classification, "and it is this emotional value which plays the significant part in the way ideas are connected and separated. It is the dominant characteristic in classification" (1963, 86).

In the introduction to Durkheim and Mauss's *Primitive Classification*, Rodney Needham challenges many of the premises of Durkheim and Mauss. First, he argues against "this unevidenced and unreasoned resort to sentiment as the ultimate explanation for the complexities of social and symbolic classification" (xxiii). He further questions sentiment as the basis for social groups, arguing instead that it is "more plausibly the *result* of such aggregation" (xxiv, emphasis added). He complains that the notion of sentiment does not explain why societies with similar structures should classify reality so differently, or why structurally different societies produce such similar classifications. Moreover, in his most serious charge, Needham sees no logical necessity for a causal connection between social structure and classification. Instead of distinguishing social order and symbolic classificatory order, Needham suggests that both are of the same order.

I agree with Needham on this last point. Social order and symbolic order are indicative of the same general propensity to classify. I also agree that Durkheim and Mauss do not show how sentiment is the basis for classification, social or symbolic. But I think the question of sentiment or affectivity and its relation to social order and classification raised by Durkheim and Mauss has not been eliminated by Needham's complaints. Needham has dismissed "sentimental affinities" because "they do not explain how it is that individuals of common psychic dispositions should engender such systematically different sentiments" (xxiii, xxiv). The reason Durkheim and Mauss are unable to answer such a challenge probably is not because they did not think of it, but because they lacked an adequate psychology, including a psychology of the unconscious. As earlier critics recognized, "Durkheim's theory of the origin of the categories depends on his ambiguous conception of mind" (xxvii).

While their conception of mind, coming as it did at the beginning of the age of psychology, may be ambiguous, Durkheim and Mauss make such a claim for "sentimental affinities" in the organization of both thought and classification based on a rather simple hypothesis: "man began to conceive things by relating them to himself" (86). If this idea is placed within a more developmental framework, human consciousness and self-consciousness take "place through participation in language, culture, institutions, and eventually the whole structure of society, [in fact,] this society becomes a constitutive element of their self-definition as persons" (Baum 1975, 131). Indeed, continues Baum, "each person encounters society as a dimension of his or her own consciousness" (131). The idea of a process of socialization through affective affinities with symbols reflects in a very crude and incomplete sense the developmental theories of both object-relations theory and self-psychology. Had Durkheim access to such theories, he might not have rejected so completely the possibility of a psychological component to his theory. Unfortunately, he insisted that "whenever a psychological explanation is given for a social phenomenon, we may be certain that it is wrong" (1938, 104).

The work of Hubert and Mauss on sacrifice is significant in the history of the theory of sacrifice because it moves beyond anthropology as catalogues of comparative morphology and begins to approach the question of what functions sacrifice serves in addition to what participants consciously might think or believe. Along with Durkheim, they interpret the ritual as somehow reflecting and legitimating social order. They also recognized the dynamic relationship between social classification and value exchange contained within a symbol.

Society is a classificatory structure, or system of such structure, fueled by affective affinities (sentiment and identification). These structures have a moral value legitimated by the sacred. The sacred realm is also a classificatory system, which in turn reflects and legitimates the social structure. The juxtaposition of the ideal sacred system with the profane social system leads to moral contradictions between the two. The function of sacrifice is to negotiate between the two realms and restore the morally correct (ideal) through a symbolic value exchange.

What Durkheim, Mauss, and Hubert fail to consider, however, is that social structure and its sacred reflection, as well as the sentiment and identification that fuel both, are grounded in social structure and culture in which *men*, and not women, sacrifice. Men control the techniques for negotiating between the sacred and the profane worlds of ritual blood sacrifice. If, as Durkheim and his students, Hubert and Mauss, argue, the sacred is a reflection of the social world, then the social world also must contain elements of this gender dichotomy. While this may seem obvious to late twentieth-century social scientists, it could not be noticed by these functionalists. Men's exclusive view of sacred and social reality legitimates their claim to the techniques of sacred *and* social power, including coercion and control, by insisting on their external facticity. As Berger and Luckmann note, "the fundamental coerciveness of society lies not in its machineries of social control, but in its power to constitute and to impose itself as reality" (1967, 12).

T w o

Claude Lévi-Strauss: The Structural
Anthropology of Classification and Sacrifice

CLAUDE LÉVI-STRAUSS acknowledges his debt to the sociological theory of Durkheim. He dedicated his first collected essays on structural anthropology to Durkheim, confessing that Durkheim's task (for the *Année Sociologique*) "would prove too much for us" (1967, x). While understanding Lévi-Strauss's own thought may prove difficult (at times I am not sure what he is saying), his structural theory and his theory of sacrifice are important. Perhaps equally important is his ambivalent relationship with psychoanalysis. I suspect that Freud's ideas fascinated him. After all, both he and Freud were driven by the same desire—to discover the essence of the human mind. Freud's psychoanalytic journey to discover the unconscious mind was paralleled by Lévi-Strauss's journey into the South American jungle for the purest form of the savage mind (*see* Lévi-Strauss 1964). And, while neither created the definitive explanation, both were highly creative, daring, and influential thinkers.

As was Freud's, Lévi-Strauss's research was fueled by his own psychological structures. He once wrote that he had never had a clear perception of his own personal identity. "I appear to myself as the place where something is going on, but there is no 'I,' no 'me'" (1978, 3). The "place" or "crossroads" where this activity occurs is "passive," happenstance; "there is no choice, it is a matter of chance" (4). The lack of a sense of what could be called a structural self might lead an individual to search for the epigenetic, psychological, and cultural structures of the human mind, which are universal, timeless, and suprapersonal. Such a search eventually influenced not only his own discipline of anthropology, but those of literary theory, linguistics, cognitive psychology, and philosophy. And although that influence may appear to be waning, Lévi-Strauss's discussion of the nature and function of sacrifice helps point out some of the key psychological issues of sacrifice. His theory of sacrifice depends on his theory of structuralism. Yet, as I argue below, for him, sacrifice is an annoying exception to a structuralism that works better with myth than with ritual.

Lévi-Strauss appears to have been intensely single-minded in his effort to discover the underlying logical structures of human consciousness and culture. The structuralism he developed presupposes the presence within human culture of binary oppositions that are logical, repeatable, transformable, and discernible. The basis for this assertion, indeed the basic supposition of structuralism, is the belief that "all social life, however elementary, presupposes an intellectual activity in man of which the formal properties cannot, accordingly, be a reflection of the concrete organization of society" (Lévi-Strauss 1963, 96). This amounts to an inversion of Durkheim's insistence on the preeminent role of the social over the psychological (or at least the cognitive). Lévi-Strauss contends that the logic of social order, manifested in classifications based on binary oppositions, is a reflection and extension of the logic of the mind itself. In his commentary on Lévi-Strauss's structuralism, Jean Piaget writes: "Behind the 'concrete social relations' there is always 'conceptual structure,' unconscious, no doubt, and therefore discoverable only by elaborating abstract structural models, but nonetheless formative" (1968, 107). At times the grandness of this theory is a bit overwhelming. In order to move safely through that theory and to keep sight of the goal— the theory of sacrifice—I have organized my discussion of Lévi-Strauss's structuralism around three interrelated ideas: (1) the idea of different modes of thought, specifically, the "savage" mode; (2) the idea of transformable binary oppositions in classification; (3) the symbolic function of a sacrificial system and its distinction from a classificatory system.

MODES OF THOUGHT

IF THE KEY to understanding social meaning lies in the discovery of conceptual structure, the key to understanding the conceptual structure lies in the discovery of the modes of human thought. By looking at the symbolic products of the savage mind, Lévi-Strauss hoped to find a way to link all the modes of thought (mythical and scientific are the two he compares most). For Lévi-Strauss there is, at least among "savages," a mode of thought that has to do with the "attention to the concrete." In *The Savage Mind* Lévi-Strauss calls this mode "the science of the concrete" (1966, 1–33). The science of the concrete is the mythical and primary mode of thought savages use to organize and, therefore, make intelligible human experience. Such thought is, according to Lévi-Strauss, "founded on this demand for order," a demand shared with all people and all modes of thought (10).

Mythical or savage thought is based on a timeless bricolage of mental structures (263). Mythical thought "expresses itself by means of a heterogeneous repertoire, which, even if extensive, is nevertheless limited" (17). This limited heterogeneous repertoire is comprised of the "remains and debris of events: . . . fossilized evidence of the history of an individual or a society" (22). Mythical thought uses this bricolage to create structures. It takes bits of the fossils, arranges and rearranges the bits, and builds on the existing or crumbling structures. Geertz likens the process to that of a kaleidoscope: "Savage logic works like a kaleidoscope whose chips can fall into a variety of patterns while remaining unchanged in quantity, form, or color. The number of patterns producible in this way may be large if the chips are numerous and varied enough, but it is not infinite. . . . And their range of possible transformations is strictly determined by the construction of the kaleidoscope, the inner law which governs its operation" (1973, 352).

Lévi-Strauss is arguing for a means of building the various cultural patterns that have ever been or ever will be based on a large but limited set of psychological and historical artifacts. These artifacts clearly seem to be of the same order as Durkheim's "*la conscience collective*" (1951, 312–20). But Lévi-Strauss takes this structural idea out of the social and historical, where Durkheim wants it, and places it within the human mind as deep, unconscious, and timeless structure, related to but distinct from the empirical world. Lévi-Strauss claims the deep structure exists because his structuralism has discovered it in the analysis of mythical thought and classificatory systems. Yet he remains vague on its exact nature.

This may be the place to introduce those elements of a dynamic psychology that would help explain the savage mind in us all, while still leaving open the question of its validity. The savage mind cannot be understood simply by using a tripartite psychoanalytic structure of the mind (id-ego-superego) because the deep, pre-existing structures are atemporal (Lévi-Strauss 1966, 198). Freud understood psychological structure as diachronic (Homans 1989, 284f). The resolution of the apparent contradiction between Lévi-Strauss's synchronic structures and Freud's diachronic structures is that the pre-existing atemporal structures Lévi-Strauss proposes would be better understood using a later psychoanalytic idea of pre-structural (or preoedipal) psychic activities, of which I will have more to say in Parts II and III. In other words, the process of bricolage, of structure building, is not simply the result of psychic drives and conflicts (as Freud would have argued), but a reflective result of psychic building—a process Freud was unable to fully delineate, although, as I argue in Chapter 6, he made a noble attempt.

TRANSFORMABLE BINARY OPPOSITION AND CLASSIFICATION

IF GEERTZ'S EXCELLENT image of the kaleidoscope is reduced to its absolute barest elements, what would be left? The most elemental structure would be that of a binary opposition. Binary opposition is the basic structure of mythical or savage thought and language. It is also the foundation of all subsequent structure. This is a central idea for Lévi-Strauss's theory. It indicates the basic structure of all savage thought, primitive classifications, and, by extension, all human thought. Binary opposition also permits the transformation of structure. "All classification proceeds by pairs of contrasts: classification only ceases when it is no longer possible to establish oppositions" (Lévi-Strauss 1966, 217). As long as opposition is possible, classification can be as ambitious as there are oppositions to name. Durkheim claimed that sentiment fuels classification. Lévi-Strauss accentuates logic and the rational. Despite this difference, Durkheim appears to anticipate, or perhaps furnish, this notion of binary opposition in classification when he writes that "when a classification is reduced to two classes, these are almost necessarily conceived as antitheses" (1915, 13).

Cultural systems of classification are based on contiguity or resemblance. But any "principle underlying a classification can never be postulated in advance" (Lévi-Strauss 1966, 58). The association and identification necessary to the construction of a classificatory system, for example a totemic or kinship system, can only be determined through the anthropological observation of native experience. And, although the logics of classification are based on association and identification, they (the logics) are "shaped by the insistence on differentiation" (75). The differentiation based on binary opposition is used by both anthropologist and native as a grid to "decipher the text [of the classification]" (75).

CLASSIFICATORY SYSTEMS AND SACRIFICIAL SYSTEMS

LÉVI-STRAUSS PRESENTS HIS system of sacrifice as the antithesis (binary opposite?) of the classificatory system, and he explains the sacrificial system in terms of the classificatory system. He begins the discussion of sacrifice by distinguishing it from totemism. Totemism, if it exists, is a form of a system of classification. Not only is that system not the origin of sacrifice, but "the two systems are mutually exclusive" (1966, 75). Totemism, as with all forms of savage classification, depends on the establishment and maintenance of a system of "differentiation between terms posited as discontinuous" (75). Discontinuity of terms, based on the principle of binary opposition, provides the structure necessary for social meaning. Sacrifice, on the other hand, seeks through substitution to establish continuity between two or more terms that are not related: "In sacrifice, the series of natural species (continuous and no longer discontinuous, oriented and no longer reversible) plays the part of an intermediary between two polar terms, the sacrificer and the deity, between which there is initially no homology nor even any sort of relation. For the object of the sacrifice is to establish a relation, not of resemblance but of contiguity, by means of a series of identifications" (224–25).

The continuity between the human plane and the divine plane is established through an intermediary victim—a pivotal species in the identification of the two planes. This identification may involve a whole series of identifications—usually a series of natural species (e.g., "of the person offering the sacrifice with the sacrificer, of the sacrificer with the victim, of the sacralized victim with the divinity; or in the reverse order") (225). The continuous identification of the two planes functions as a form of communication. The destruction

of the victim sets off a desired effect from the divine plane. The ambiguous victim, being in both planes, is destroyed in order to break
the continuity. Yet the destruction also releases the desired divine
communication. Presented with this apparent contradiction, Lévi-
Strauss concludes that sacrifice "represents a private discourse want-
ing in good sense for all that it may frequently be pronounced" (228).

The basis for the distinction between a classificatory system and
a sacrificial system has to do with the way that the series of natural
species operate within each system. In classification the series is a
homology (it is metaphorical); in sacrifice it is a series of identifications (it is metonymical). Lévi-Strauss further distinguishes the two
by claiming that sacrifice is a private discourse, while classification,
as a product of language, is a social phenomenon. This latter distinction is ethnographically incorrect. For example, in his study of
the Dinka, Godfrey Lienhardt states that "no theory of sacrifice which
neglects the fact that the act is primarily social can therefore be of
service in interpreting the sacrifices of the Dinka" (1961, 292). Lévi-
Strauss seems to be using the term *private* to indicate that sacrifice
does not make sense in the same way language (classificatory system)
does.

However much Lévi-Strauss uses binary opposition in an effort
to see the non-conflicting wholeness of the mind and culture, the
psychology of sacrifice confounds him. He cannot make any sense
out of it and even seems annoyed with rituals of sacrifice. I suspect
that his reluctance to venture any further into the apparent illogical
psychology of sacrifice has to do with his structural point of view,
with its emphasis on the logical structure of oppositional, intentional,
and ideational thought, concepts that do not lend themselves as well
to the analysis of action (ritual) as to words (cultural classification
and myth). Moreover, having insisted that classification aids thought
by establishing distinction and that sacrifice eliminates distinction,
his point of view does not allow him to explore the dialectical relationship between the two symbolic modes of classification and sacrifice. Yet, to a certain degree he presents evidence for such a relationship between classification and sacrifice.

Lévi-Strauss remarks that sacrifice "resembles, though it is at
the same time opposed to them, the rites termed 'sacrilegious,' such
as incest, bestiality, etc." He states that sacrifice is an "*extreme* operation which relates to an *intermediary* object [while] . . . incest,
bestiality . . . are *intermediary* operations relating to *extreme* objects"

(1966, 225). He seems to suggest that sacrifice resembles incest in an inverse way, or perhaps even that sacrifice is an inverse form of incest. For Lévi-Strauss incest (or rather the incest taboo) is fundamental to one of the most important classificatory systems in human society: kinship. "The primitive and irreducible character of the basic unit of kinship, as I have defined it, is actually a direct result of the universal presence of an incest taboo" (1967, 44; *see* 1969, 488–90). What he seems to be thinking, even if he has not written it, is that both sacrifice and kinship (classificatory) systems oppose incest. They are alike in this regard. They are also alike in that they are both constructions of the mind at an unconscious level.

Taking this discussion a bit further, Lévi-Strauss states in another essay that the incest taboo is one of "many different ways of insuring the circulation of women within the social group or of substituting the mechanism of a sociologically determined affinity for that of a biologically determined consanguinity" (1967, 59). The incest taboo allows for the peaceful circulation of women within and between different male groups. He suggests that women have meaning in society in much the same way words (or phonemes) do in language. Of course he is aware of the charge of "anti-feminism" that could be leveled against his apparent reduction of women to objects (60). This discussion occurs within the context of an analysis of language and kinship, in which he is trying to indicate the similarities between the exchange of complementary values in the exchange of both women and words. He is asking "whether there are not only 'operational' but also 'substantial comparabilities' between language and culture" (61). Some feminists have recognized the value of his insight and question (*see* Mitchell 1974).

Sacrifice not only opposes incest, thereby resembling the function of the incest taboo and kinship systems, it also resembles incest. I am somewhat straining the work of Lévi-Strauss when I suggest that there is a relationship between sacrifice and incest that has to do with the control of women. Sacrifice's "obsession with blood" has something to do with controlling consanguineous women. But Lévi-Strauss does not acknowledge this relationship. He sees the comparability of language and kinship, but comparing sacrifice and kinship seems hopeless to him. The unconscious structure of language is logical; the unconscious structure of sacrifice is illogical and obsessional to Lévi-Strauss, and he cannot hope to discover that structure as long as he fails to recognize who is sacrificing and how the sacrificer is connected to consanguineous women. Lévi-Strauss has asked anthropological questions for which he has no psychological answers. His interpretations must remain at the symbolic and metaphorical level. For example, he notes that "there is an empirical connection between marriage rules and eating prohibitions," seen in the analogy between copulation and eating (incest and cannibalism being the "most exaggerated forms") (1966, 104–5). Yet Lévi-Strauss contends that the connection between them is metaphorical and not causal, psychological or otherwise.

I believe Lévi-Strauss has attempted as an anthropologist to develop a psychology that Freud, as a psychoanalyst, also was unable to develop. I want to close this discussion of Lévi-Strauss by suggesting the direction for a psychological resolution of his dilemma about sacrifice and classification. Classifications lend themselves well to the working of the savage mind—the science of the concrete. Sacrifice does not lend itself as well. For Lévi-Strauss, sacrifice is a failure of the science of the concrete. Why? Perhaps sacrifice fails because it is a diachronic act and thus beyond the synchronic and mythical. In this sense, sacrifice breaks the synchronic web of the atemporal savage mind and sets the social world in history (time). This would not be far from where Freud landed in *Totem and Taboo* (1913). But, perhaps sacrifice is somehow pre-structural and thus somehow "pre-chronic," in the sense of being pre-historical and pre-mythical. To paraphrase Goethe, in the beginning was not the *word* but the *act* of sacrifice. Understood this way, sacrifice breaks down the metaphorical classificatory logic and leads to a relation with the sacred outside the category of time altogether. Synchronic, mythical thought comes into existence with language, with structure. The movement from synchrony to diachrony, from myth to history is an option Lévi-Strauss rightly rejects. Synchrony exists even with the development of history. But the capacity for mythical and historical thought may reside within a deep, pre-structural dimension of the mind that Lévi-Strauss, as an anthropologist, could not perceive in myth and classification because its "logic" resides in illogical acts such as sacrifice. To begin to understand the pre-structures behind both myth and ritual, I will need to gain a deeper sense of the nature of the symbolic in the mind and in culture. Gaining a sense of the symbolic in culture has been the task of both Mary Douglas and Victor Turner, to whom I now turn.

THREE

The Symbolic Anthropology of Ritual

SYMBOLIC ANTHROPOLOGY IS the study of symbols as instigators and receptacles of social contradiction and social action. The two best-known, articulate proponents of this kind of anthropology are Mary Douglas and Victor Turner. Critics have argued that by placing the symbol at the center of anthropological analysis, Douglas and Turner avoid "the clash between symbol and structure" (Barrett 1984, 209). Social structure contains evident contradictions, which symbolic rit-uals attempt to neutralize. That is, ritual is a response to social struc-tural contradictions. Barrett sees an early Turner exploring the layers of social structural contradictions hidden within levels of ritual and symbol (*see* Turner 1967). Barrett then laments that a later Turner gave "ritual symbol the centre of the stage and attributing indepen-dent causal status to it" (Barrett 1984, 208). Like Geertz, Turner contends that "symbols instigate social action" (Turner 1969, 55). Barrett goes on to include Douglas in this indictment. By giving the symbol the central role in the creation of social norms and values, Turner and Douglas avoid this clash between the symbol and struc-ture. My reading of Douglas and Turner does not support such a criticism. Barrett assumes too large a distinction between structure and symbol, that is, between social structure and culture. If anything, Douglas, Turner, and even Geertz prove to be problematic for "di-alectical anthropology" (Barrett 1984), not because they present a homology between belief and action, but because the symbol *does* play a significant role in the social construction of reality (both social structure and culture). As I argue below, Douglas and Turner do not lose sight of structural conflicts and contradictions, which symbols initiate, conceal, and transform. The limitations of Douglas and Turner lie in their awareness of psychological processes in the creation of symbol (both Douglas and Turner struggle with giving credence to psychodynamics evident to them in both symbolic action and social structure), and their reluctance to choose an explanatory psychodynamic point of view.

MARY DOUGLAS: BOUNDARIES AND DANGER

MARY DOUGLAS INTERPRETS Durkheim's theory of the sacred as "a theory about how knowledge of the universe is socially constructed" (1975, xiv). In her work on the meaning of ritual she is concerned with the structure of the socially constructed sacred and with how it is recognized. Like Lévi-Strauss she maintains that human beings have an innate proclivity to classify experience into discrete phenomena. Because of this tendency, they continue to impose transformable symbolic patterns on inherently messy experience. This messiness or ambiguity, when it is recognized, is often experienced as dangerous. Ambiguity shares this danger with the sacred. "The first essential character by which the sacred is recognizable is its dangerousness" (xv).

The innate proclivity to classify experience does not, however, preclude the social imposition of meaning or its structure on classification. In fact, classificatory boundaries are constructed around the sacred in order to protect the social consensus. "The only one who holds nothing sacred," writes Douglas, "is the one who has not internalised the norms of any community" (xv). Here Douglas is following Durkheim. Whereas Lévi-Strauss argues for innate structures within the mind to account for the patterns of religious symbols and meaning, Douglas maintains that "the reasons for any particular way of defining the sacred are embedded in the social consensus which it protects" (xv). Thus, when this messiness or ambiguity (the sacred contagion) appears, it is dangerous to the existing cultural patterns because it threatens structural classifications of reality, that is, the inclusive structures of society.

Danger to such inclusive classifications can occur in four ways: (1) The danger can be in the form of external pressure on the boundaries of cultural structures. The structures may have internal integrity but experience is made up of many elements, which may not be part of a cultural system. Hence, there are always possible threats from outside the system. (2) The structure may be threatened by internal factors exerting pressure within structural boundaries. (3) The danger can result from the ambiguity of the boundaries themselves; i.e., Where does the system begin and end? (4) Finally, the danger can result from the tension or contradiction between two elements within the structural boundaries (136). Whatever the form of danger, the significant factor is that the danger is found within marginal states or marginal people. To move across boundaries is to move into margins; it is to move into danger and to be at a source of power. Douglas states that the "power which presents a danger for careless humans is very evidently in the structure of ideas, a power from which the structure is expected to protect itself" (1966, 122).

Douglas demonstrates this quality of marginality by using the human body. The human body can be understood as the mediator between the individual and the external environment. Everything within the body is part of the individual; everything outside is part of the environment. The body orifices represent transitional zones where various substances either enter (food, milk, water, wine, semen) or leave (urine, feces, spittle, milk, blood, tears, semen). These substances transverse the boundaries of the body and can be experienced as dangerous, polluting, and powerful—depending on the specific culture. For example, in some cultures menstrual blood is feared as a polluting danger; in others there is no concern about it at all.

The symbolic significance of the transitional or marginal zones is their threat to culturally determined classification patterns, symbolized by the human body. Because these disturbances to social structures do occur, they are often incorporated into the social patterns and at least consciously are accepted as normative. Yet ritualized anomalies remain potentially contagious and therefore dangerous. The socially learned reaction to marginal states, which Douglas discovered in her field work with the Lele (a tropical jungle culture of central Africa), involves two related terms: *buhonyi* and *hama*. *Buhonyi* "provides the standards of all social relations" (1975, 10). Douglas translates the word as a combination of shame, shyness, and modesty. *Hama* is anything that inspires disgust or anything that is disgusting or dreaded or makes one anxious.

For Douglas, one of the primary functions of ritual is to allow for the transition "across" the contagion that lies between classificatory boundaries. Ritual accomplishes this by allowing the ambiguous tension to be focused on and resolved within a framed structure, which brackets the ambiguity and keeps it from polluting the unified cultural patterns. In this way ritual serves to avoid potential, or overcome actual, danger. In the example of the symbolism of the human body, various rituals can allow bodily fluids to pass from one classification to another without disturbing the larger cultural pattern. The same holds true for sacrifice. Drawing on Lienhardt's field work, Douglas notes that the Dinka have any number of ways of sacrificing an animal depending on the desired intention. Lienhardt (1961) maintains the Durkheimian position that ritual creates and controls experience; its purpose is to reinforce the normative. In the best-known example, cancellation of an incest violation is accomplished by cutting the animal in half lengthwise, including the genitals. "What is being carved upon the body of the animal," writes Douglas, "is a division to be recognized in future between two lineages: formerly they begot children in one line, now they are divided as to begetting: hence the cut through the genital organs" (1975, 67–68). The body of the animal is an image of the social body. Douglas claims that the same interpretation can be made with regard to carving up the human body as well. "This is a central clue to the incision rites which use womb envy to express something about the constitution of society" (68). If that is the case, then the blood of the sacrificial animal is correlative to blood that occurs as a part of the social structure, the most obvious being menstrual blood and all that it signifies.

Douglas has developed a mode of interpretation that is well argued. It is also useful in the articulation of a revised psychoanalytic theory of sacrifice. She is sensitive to insights made by psychoanalysis and even takes advantage of that insight in developing her theory of ritual. In describing the bracketing or framing of experience that ritual accomplishes, Douglas makes reference to Marion Milner's (1955) essay on symbol formation. However, Douglas chooses not to move very far from her Durkheimian position. The sacrificial body of an ox symbolizes the body politic. She is unwilling to take the same step Lévi-Strauss took and claim that the body politic is an external expression of deep mental structures. But are the only options Durkheim's or Lévi-Strauss's? Douglas chose to study a society that has no lineages and, not unrelated to the absence of lineages, practices no sacrifice. There continues to be discussion among anthropologists as to whether the killing of the pangolin, an armadillo-type animal of Africa and Asia, is a sacrifice. In de Heusch's (1985) structural study of African sacrifice, this killing is "a somewhat sacrilegious sacrifice," " a quasi-sacrificial dissection" (29, 30). In spite of the ambiguity, or perhaps because of it, Douglas provides several insights helpful in understanding sacrifice. She furthers an understanding of the relationship between social systems of classification and marginality. She also explores more fully than previous anthropologists the relationship between marginality and affect in her analysis of anxiety, danger, *hama* and *buhonyi*. Interestingly, the pangolin promotes female fertility (Douglas 1975, 55) and is "the only animal capable of feeling shame (*buhonyi*)" (de Heusch 1985, 29). But Douglas resists interpreting the learned affect about the pangolin and that affect's relation to a psychodynamic apparatus. She is correct in asserting that the anxiety involved in margins is not, for example, anxiety about body orifices or expressions of common infantile fantasies. Rather, anxiety expresses the care to protect an existing differentiated social structure. Yet she simply takes for granted this type of anxiety. She does not ask: Why does dedifferentiation lead to anxiety? What is the loss of prestige or order or power or image all about psychologically? Of course her familiarity with psychoanalytic theory is limited to the classical drive model (which even the British object relations school, including Milner, does not completely abandon). These earlier theories, however, do not answer the questions Douglas raised. As with Freud's theory of the uncanny (*see* chapter 6), *buhonyi* and *hama* do not fit nicely into a classical psychoanalytic theory. They could, however, fit into a self-psychological one, and I shall return to this in chapter 11.

Victor Turner: Experience, Liminality, and Ritual Symbol

In discussing the work of Lévi-Strauss, Clifford Geertz writes that structural anthropology, that "infernal culture machine[,] . . . annuls history, reduces sentiment to a shadow of the intellect, and replaces the particular mind of particular savages in particular jungles with the Savage Mind immanent in us all" (1973, 355). Victor Turner makes an effort to move beyond this synchronic structuralism to understand symbols and rituals contextualized within social processes and spatiotemporal continua. Unlike other British and French anthropologists whose structural-functional orientation seems to elevate social *or* mental structures at the expense of the actual human participants, Turner sought to analyze and interpret human action as a process or experience. Referred to as processual symbolic analysis or the anthropology of experience, this mode of analysis focuses on those cultural symbols (dominant symbols, symbolic rituals) that "mediate between individual unconscious impulses and intentions and the social processes of the group making for its cohesion and continuity" (Turner 1985, 126). Moreover, unlike Lévi-Strauss, Turner does not choose to discount observed social conflict with an appeal to universal and unifying deep structures. In his field work with Ndembu society, Turner observed "the real interconnections and conflicts between groups and persons," as they are represented in ritual (1967, 27).

The anthropology of experience seeks the relationship between social drama and the ritual process, a relationship which indicates that an entire experience of individual, social, and ritual action is interconnected. This emphasis on process does not preclude the importance of structure. In fact, "process is intimately bound up with structure and . . . an adequate analysis of social life necessitates a rigorous consideration of the relation between them" (1985, 156). This is the task of anthropology, and Turner understands it as part of a larger human science in which other disciplines are both acceptable and necessary. While some of his colleagues found his increasing interest in neurobiology, for example, to be a reductionistic threat, from a psychoanalytic anthropological point of view, Turner's acceptance of ritual affect as having an orectic and unconscious dimension has been encouraging. I want briefly to outline his theory of social drama and ritual process and focus on three elements of that theory—social crisis, ritual passage, and liminality—as a way of presenting a Turner theory of sacrifice.

Social drama evolves through four recognizably distinct stages: breach, crisis, redressive process, and either reintegration or recognition of irreparable schism. A breach results from rule breaking. The breach may also occur as a part of the social maturational process of an individual or group, or as a result of disease, birth, death, or combination of any of the above. The importance of the breach is not simply that a social pattern or structure is disturbed, but that the breach is *experienced*. Here Turner's idea of experience, particularly at the breach level, is taken from Wilhelm Dilthey, who distinguished between mere "experience" and "an experience" (Dilthey 1976, 210). Turner elaborates:

> Each of us has had certain "experiences" which have been form-
> ative and transformative, that is, distinguishable, isolatable se-
> quences of external events and internal responses to them such
> as initiations into new lifeways (going to school, first job, join-
> ing the army, entering the marital status), love affairs, being caught
> up in some model of what Emile Durkheim called "social ef-
> fervescence" (a political campaign, a declaration of war, a cause
> célèbre such as the Dreyfus Affair, Watergate, the Iranian hos-
> tage crisis, or the Russian Revolution). Some of these formative
> experiences are highly personal, others are shared with groups
> to which we belong by birth or choice. Dilthey saw such ex-
> periences as having a temporal or processual structure—they
> "processed" through distinguishable stages. . . . Moreover, they
> involved in their structuring at every moment and phase not
> simply *thought* structuring but the whole human vital repertoire
> of thinking, willing, desiring, and feeling, subtly and varyingly
> interpenetrating on many levels. . . .
>
> These experiences that erupt from or disrupt routinized, re-
> petitive behavior . . . summon up precedents and likenesses from
> the conscious and unconscious past. (1985, 35–36)

The eruption experience forms the breach in the normative structural
patterns of social life. The social structure is itself "provocative of
competition and conflict, even as it restrains its public expression"
(Turner 1985, 232). This breach, in which mere experience is inten-
sified by affective meaning, spreads through the social group because
of its dissonance, leading to the second stage of the social drama, the
crisis. As social disequilibrium becomes more pronounced, there is a
structural need and social demand for redressive action—the third
stage. The redressive process may take three different forms. There
may be a political process or a legal-judicial process. Or there may
be a ritual process. As the central structure of ritual, Turner takes
Arnold van Gennep's scheme in *Rites of Passage* (1960), in which
there are rites of separation, rites of limen or margin, and rites of
reaggregation. It is not overly important to make distinctions between rites of passage, rites of intensification, rites of affliction, or
the like, because all of them express the element of liminality—the
key to understanding ritual.

Within the three-part structure of ritual, Turner focuses his efforts on the central rite—the rite of limen or margin. In an earlier
article, Turner (1964) first spells out the qualities of liminality, the
very essence (meaning and value) of ritual. He later includes these

ideas in his book *The Ritual Process*, in which he writes: "The attributes of liminality or of liminal *personae* ("threshold people") are necessarily ambiguous, since this condition and these persons elude or slip through the network of classifications that normally locate states and positions in cultural space. Liminal entities are neither here nor there; they are betwixt and between the positions assigned and arranged by law, custom, convention, and ceremonial" (1969, 95). In the ritual process, liminality is the ambiguous, transitional stage between more formal states or positions. Liminality can be expressed through a multitude of diverse symbolism because the imagination is less restrained, more free. Since it is "betwixt and between," liminality is often compared to "death, to being in the womb, to invisibility, to darkness, to bisexuality, to the wilderness, and to eclipses of the sun and moon" (95).

Turner notes two interrelated consequences of liminality and the liminal period in ritual. First, liminality has the effect of *eliminating* (literally, 'from the threshold') previous social identity and distinctions in order to prepare the participants for their new station in social life. And second, such elimination has the consequence of drawing the participants closer together. That is, with the social structures (e.g., kinship, status) gone, the participants share a common identity, purpose, and space. This liminal community is unstructured and more or less undifferentiated. Turner defines the liminal experience of the participants as "communitas." He distinguishes communitas from structure. Indeed, communitas is "anti-structure" (96–97). The social purpose of communitas within liminality is to allow the participants, no matter what their social status, to experience the reality that all are in communion, that the higher need the lower, and that the opposites, as it were, constitute one another and are mutually indispensable. The effect of communitas is to allow the ritual process to proceed to reaggregation. Then, returning to the four-part social drama, the reintegration of the participants into the larger society is finally able to take place.

Having briefly outlined the main themes of the ritual process (with emphasis on crisis and liminality/communitas), I want to examine the properties of the ritual symbols and how they express liminality. Turner states that the multifocal nature of ritual symbol has three essential properties of which the interpreter needs to be aware. The first and "simplest property is that of *condensation*" (1967, 28). A whole range of things (action, affect, observation, social reality, etc.) can be represented or condensed into a single unit of expression. Related to the idea of condensation is that "a dominant (i.e, a culturally primal) symbol is a *unification of disparate significata*" (28). The third property of symbols is "polarization of meaning" (29). Turner maintains that a dominant or master ritual symbol expresses both the unconscious desires and intentions of individuals and the social order or ideology of the group. Thus, the condensation of disparate significata occurs along a continuum of orectic/sensory and ideological poles of meaning. At the sensory pole the meaning expresses an outward, perhaps visible, form of the symbol. For example, during Ndembu male circumcision rites, the master symbol prior to circumcision is *Mudyi*, the "milk tree." Following circumcision, the master symbol is *Mukula*, the "red tree." Both *Mudyi* and *Mukula* are master symbols that are multifocal—a continuum of meaning between sensory and normative poles. Take *Mukula*. At its sensory, orectic, or physiological pole, *Mukula* represents different types of blood: blood from a hunted animal, maternal birthing blood, menstrual blood, the blood of circumcision. At the normative or ideological pole, however, the *Mukula* represents matriliny, a quality of social structure, "associated with sentiments of solidarity, reciprocity, loyalty" (Turner 1978, 574–75). Such sentiments included "obligations to perpetuate matrilineage" through a particular womb group (575). Circumcision represents the symbolic movement from male childhood to manhood, *Mudyi* representing first the milk of the mother and then the white semen of manhood. *Mukula* represents the maternal blood and then the blood of the male hunter. At the normative pole, *Mudyi* represents solidarity with the mother and then male solidarity. *Mukula* represents matrilineal solidarity and then male hunting solidarity. The symbolic movement from *Mudyi* to *Mukula* represents a movement from mother to matrilineal yet patrifocal structure. Because of the properties of symbols, disparate significata of the circumcision ritual can occupy the same meaning space, expressing both the sensory and ideological poles of the symbol.

Turner, like Mary Douglas, studied an African society. For the Ndembu, sacrifice is not a dominant ritual symbol. However, parts of the Ndembu ritual process could, in Turner's opinion, be considered sacrificial. From his processual point of view, sacrifice instigates and mediates the conflicts of various socially liminal dramas. Sacrifice is a process that expresses the abandonment (meaning destructuring) of a previous state and the prophylaxis (or restructuring) of the new state (1977). A sacrifice signifies a form of liminality in the body of the victim. It also marks the separation from that state. In the liminal state there is a reduction of distinctions, a dedifferentiation of the participants. For this to be possible, the previous (preliminal) state is emphasized, symbolized by the soon-to-be-dead body of the victim. Death represents the end of the former state, which had to occur before the new state can come into social existence. Jay (1985) notes that the two states represented in the ritual sacrifice discussed by Turner are those of the matriliny (the abandoned state) and patriliny (the restructured state). Although Turner fails to take account of this, he shows quite clearly that a ritual such as sacrifice expresses and contains social conflict and structural contradiction.

Both Douglas and Turner develop theories of symbol and ritual that lend themselves quite well to object-relations and other post-Freudian psychoanalytic thought. Douglas's analysis of boundaries, danger, and ritual has remarkable affinities with Klein's (1963) understanding of symbol formation and ego development (*see* Chapter 8). And Turner's analysis of communitas and liminality works nicely with Winnicott's (1971a) idea of the transitional object and play (Ross and Ross 1983, a somewhat optimistic psychoanalytic view of ritual). I shall return to the ideas of boundaries and transitions in Part II.

F O U R

Clifford Geertz: Ritual as a Cultural System

EACH OF THE previous anthropological perspectives have acknowledged and responded to psychological questions manifest in its analysis of ritual and sacrifice. Durkheim is the least comfortable with acknowledging the unconscious, Lévi-Strauss appears to be the most ambivalent, Turner the most consistent, and Douglas perhaps the most informed. In this chapter, I show how Clifford Geertz comes very close to describing the psychodynamics of ritual sacrifice without actually attempting a psychological interpretation. In his analysis of Balinese ritual and cockfights, Geertz brings his brand of cultural anthropology into close contact with elements of dynamic psychology. In order to observe and understand cultural affect, he is not satisfied with simply stating that a ritual symbol expresses a social contradiction or conflict. He seeks to understand the affective quality of contradiction and conflict, particularly as it is embodied in ritual.

Significant symbols are clustered together into "cultural patterns," through which "man makes sense of the events through which he lives" (Geertz 1973, 363). Of particular importance is Geertz's analysis of the patterns of normative behavior in Bali, which reflect the depersonalizing patterns of person characterization and the detemporalization or "immobilization of time" (398). Geertz struggles to characterize that conduct: "it is very difficult to communicate to someone who has not experienced it." He suggests that it reflects a "playful theatricality," which is at the same time solemn and radically aesthetic and which has as its main designation that of pleasing—

but pleasing "as beauty pleases, not as virtue pleases" (400). This is as true of ritual as it is of other modes of normative behavior.

Having said this, Geertz goes on to indicate the two most important aspects of Balinese affect: *lek* and "absence of climax" (400). While claiming that he is not interested in the psychodynamics of *lek*, he does try to distinguish the Balinese term from the English terms *guilt* and *shame* because of its aesthetic rather than ethical (moral) quality. Geertz's complaint that previous studies of guilt and shame fail to sufficiently distinguish shame from guilt is a bit overzealous. A strict psychodynamic distinction between guilt and shame leads to a disruption in the theoretical continuity of the superego and the ego ideal. Consequences for such theoretical disruption were first aired by Hartmann and Lowenstein (1964) and more recently by Kohut (1978, 442). In order to distance himself from any further psychological considerations, Geertz proposes the theatrical term *stage fright* rather than shame to preserve the aesthetic quality of *lek*. His knowledge of dynamic psychology would lead him correctly to reject a drive theory of shame (an ethically harsh superego reacting to id transgressions): *lek* "has nothing to do with transgressions" (Geertz 1973, 401). But resorting to a theatrical metaphor does not resolve the psychological question of *lek*. If Geertz's phenomenological analysis is correct, how might the psychodynamics of aesthetic shame be explained? In other words, since the phenomenology (Geertz's "thick description") of *lek* contradicts Freudian theory, what psychology is available that can take into account the psychological state Geertz characterizes as aesthetic, serious, and playful, which has as its foremost task that of pleasing and which is subjectively characterized as "a diffuse, usually mild, though in certain situations virtually paralyzing, nervousness before the prospect (and fact) of social interaction, a chronic, mostly low-grade worry that one will not be able to bring it off with the required finesse"? (402).

Lek shows many similarities with what Mary Douglas describes as *buhonyi* and *hama* in her studies of the Lele. *Buhonyi* "provides the standards of all social relations" (Douglas 1975, 10). Douglas translates the word as a combination of shame, shyness, and modesty. *Hama* is anything that inspires disgust or anything that is disgusting or dreaded or makes one anxious. Geertz, like Douglas, is describing normative affect, which might be explained better through Kohut's theory of narcissism than Freud's drive theory.

In his analysis of the named categories for a person (personal names, birth names, kinship names, teknonyms, cultural status, and finally public titles), Geertz discovered that the "paradox of Balinese formulations of personhood is that they are—in our terms anyway—depersonalizing" (1973, 390). When the personhood titles are looked at as a whole, a cultural pattern is evident, and the effect is one of distancing people from each other and from divinity. For example, with teknonyms an individual is perceived "in the context of whom he is ancestral to" (379). This has the effect of keeping the individual within "an unperishing present" (379). The individual is not thought of in terms of family history or from whom the individual is descended. The individual remains contemporary because time and history stand still. Depersonalization happens with other titles as well. Personal names are usually kept secret while status and public titles reflect a distancing from divinity. Thus, along with the unperishing present, the names reflect a diminishing of intimacy with each other and with their divinity. The normative affect of *lek* is the mood that insures the depersonal and dampens intimacy.

The lack of climax expresses the cultural insistence on contemporal and motionless present in daily and ritual life. The teknonym is not the only cultural expression of the unperishing present. Most public conduct is seen as depersonalizing, lessening intimacy, and maintaining the sense of the constant contemporary. This is the affective result of reducing temporal movement and giving conduct the quality of what Geertz calls "an absence of climax." "Balinese social life lacks climax because it takes place in a motionless present, a vectorless now" (404). I want briefly to describe a Balinese ritual complex which expresses these affects as a means of discovering in an anthropological description the psychological questions I am seeking to answer..

In this ritual performance/dance, the "cast" consists of the two main mythical characters, Barong and Rangda, and to some degree the crowds of people watching and participating in the battle between Barong and Rangda. The monster Barong, who is childlike, clumsy, and silly in his exaggerated grandiosity, and the witch Rangda, evoking dread, animosity, revulsion, horror, and sadism, engage in a confused and ineffectual struggle, which reaches neither climax nor resolution. The two creatures, large costumed creations in which two or more people operate the head, body, and legs, engage in a mock battle. The performance may go on for hours as Barong (who "prances about in paroxysms of narcissistic vanity") and Rangda ("depicted as a wasted widow, a prostitute, and eater of infants") struggle endlessly for dominance (114–16). During the performance any number of participants/observers may become entranced. Geertz describes a typical performance:

> The performance begins with the appearance of Barong, prancing and preening, as a general prophylactic against what is to follow. Then may come various mythic scenes relating the story—not always precisely the same ones—upon which the performance is based, until finally Barong and then Rangda appear. Their battle begins. Barong drives Rangda back toward the gate of the death temple [a death temple celebration being the usual, but not always, location of this performance]. But he has not the power to expel her completely, and he is in turn driven back toward the village. At length, when it seems as though Rangda will finally prevail, a number of entranced men rise, krisses [knives] in hand, and rush to support Barong. But as they approach Rangda (who has turned back in meditation), she wheels upon them and, waving her *sakti* white cloth, leaves them comatose on the ground. Rangda then hastily retires (or is carried) to the temple, where she herself collapses, hidden from the aroused crowd which, my informants said, would kill her were it to see her in a helpless state. The Barong moves among the kris dancers and wakens them by snapping his jaws at them or nuzzling them with his beard. As they return, still entranced, to "consciousness," they are enraged by the disappearance of Rangda, and unable to attack her they turn their krisses (harmlessly because they are entranced) against their own chests in frustration. Usually sheer pandemonium breaks out at this point with members of the crowd, of both sexes, falling into trance all around the courtyard and rushing out to stab themselves, wrestle with one another, devour live chicks or excrement, wallow convulsively in the mud, and so on, while the nonentranced attempt to relieve them of their krisses and keep them at least minimally in order. In time, the trancers sink, one by one, into coma, from which they are aroused by the priests' holy water and the great battle is over—once more a complete stand-off. Rangda has not been conquered, but neither has she conquered (117).

The dance clearly exemplifies in the commingling of hilarity and horror, in desire and disgust, a pervading ambivalent and aesthetic anxiety. The performance seems to express a desire for extravagant self-exposure, a dread of such exposure (*lek*), and the unresolvable tension between the desire and the dread (insured by the "lack of climax").

Geertz claims that the meaning of the Rangda-Barong dance is not simply to be found in the myths and legends the dance enacts, rather in the encounter with the chief characters. It is in the encounter that "the villager comes to know them as, so far as he is concerned, genuine realities. They are, then, not representations of anything, but presences. And," concludes Geertz, "when the villagers go into the trance they become—*nadi*—themselves part of the realm in which those presences exist" (118).

This becoming "part of the realm" is very similar to Turner's view of liminality and communitas. Indeed, writes Geertz, "to become entranced is . . . to cross a threshold [limen] into another order of existence" (116). The "genuine realities" of the Rangda-Barong dance are dread (the fear and lust of Rangda) and playful, exhibitionistic grandiosity (Barong). But Rangda is not simply a representation of dread, the uncanny commingling of desire and fear; she is Dread itself, which the villagers experience in their entranced state in which they do the most dreadful (un-*lek*-like) things (Geertz does not mention the sexual activities, but he assures us they are there as well). The same is true of the presence of the comic narcissism of Barong. Geertz claims that "the comic spirit—a distinctive combination of playfulness, exhibitionism, and extravagant love of elegance, . . . along with fear, is perhaps the dominant motive in their life" (118).

Geertz is doing something fundamentally different from the functionalists (Durkheim or Lévi-Strauss) or the symbolists (Douglas or Turner). Religion and ritual do not simply inscribe or reflect social structure, nor do they merely express or create conflicts symbolically. Geertz is arguing that rituals such as the Rangda-Barong battle *shape* the social order; they shape the conflicts in society (119). Rituals also contribute to social change (142–69).

Geertz does not, however, give up his anthropological heritage or methodology. He is clear that the "system of meanings embodied in the symbols" is the place where the anthropologist begins the study of religion. It is from this system that the social and psychological processes flow—both in the individual participants and in the theories about them. Thus, in a theory of sacrifice, the ritual expresses something social and something psychological, but that ritual also helps create that something. There is, in other words, an experiential "presence" connecting the ritual to the social order and the psychological apparatus.

Geertz's fascinating insight into ritual as a cultural system does not include an explicit theory of sacrifice—at least I have not found it. I believe that his anthropological point of view, however, is applicable to such a theory. He clearly sees sacrifice as distinct from less violent rituals. "The sorts of moods and motivations which characterize a man who has just come from an Aztec human sacrifice are rather different from those of one who has just put off his Kachina mask [Zuni]" (122–23). In his own field work, Geertz claims that the Balinese cockfight is "a blood sacrifice offered, with the appropriate chants and oblations, to the demons in order to pacify their ravenous, cannibal hunger" (420). I want to spend some time now seeing how Geertz understands the "deep play" of dread and exhibitionism (dialectically related in the motivation of male prestige and self-esteem) as they are played out in the cockfight.

Geertz indicates through a double entendre that the "deep psychological identification of Balinese men with their cocks is unmistakable." Moreover, "in line with the Balinese conception of the body as a set of separately animated parts, cocks are viewed as detachable, self-operating penises, ambulant genitals with a life of their own" (417). But the identification encompasses more than the metaphorical. The relationship between a man and his cock provides a significant means of experiencing the reverse side of a culture qualified and motivated by *lek* (dread) and status: animality.

The idea of animality is on the one hand absolutely abhorrent to the Balinese (for example, for the crime of incest, one is forced to live like an animal; for bestiality, the perpetrator is drowned). Yet clearly the lure towards it, channelled through the cock, is equally undeniable. By identifying with his cock, a man identifies with a dark side of himself—"what he most fears, hates, and ambivalence being what it is, is fascinated by—'The Powers of Darkness'" (420). "In the cockfight, man and beast, good and evil, ego and id, the creative power of aroused masculinity and the destructive power of loosened animality fuse in a bloody drama of hatred, cruelty, violence, and death" (420–21). While this is one of the better anthropological definitions of sacrifice, the psychological elements of it, as suggested by Geertz's use of the Freudian ego-id dialectic, could be broadened to define the notion of "aroused masculinity" as male narcissism. But this point can best be made after a more thorough look at Kohut's theory of narcissism.

The fights take place in a ring. Geertz notices that the spectators pretend not to be interested in how the individual matches are determined, handicapped, or how the main betting odds are set. This seems to be in keeping with the typical Balinese propensity for aesthetic indirectness. Once the match is determined and main odds set, the secondary betting takes place and increases in fury until the pounding of a slit gong announces the start of the fight. The two cocks, with steel spurs attached to their legs, fight until a wound is inflicted. Then they are pulled apart and their handlers attend to them, dressing the wounds and trying to keep the cock alive for the subsequent rounds. The cock that outlives the other wins.

Through an elaborate betting system, odds are determined and made between individuals in the crowd around the ring. If the center bet (between the two groups supporting the cock owners) is high, it means that there is more at stake—better quality cocks, less predictability, more money. With more at stake in the center, the secondary betting increases as well. Such matches are, in the Balinese term, more interesting; they are "deeper." Why certain matches take on this deeper interest has to do with the social-psychological realm of identification and status. "In deep ones, where the amounts of money are great, much more is at stake than material gain: namely, esteem, honor, dignity, respect—in a word, though in Bali a profoundly freighted word, status" (433). This happens through "the migration of the Balinese status hierarchy into the body of the cockfight" (436). Because prestige is possibly the main motivational force in the society, the cockfight is "a status bloodbath" (436).

To see what "status hierarchy" is operating (who is seeking to increase prestige at the same time he is seeking to insult his opponent), I need to back away a bit from this bloody pit of male narcissism. The Balinese village in which the cockfight Geertz is describing takes place is controlled by four patrilineal descent groups, which are constantly vying with each other. The village is also endogamous and unites for all cockfights with other villages. Thus, when the fights are within the village, the betting, whether in the center or in the secondary, follows kinship loyalties. A man would not bet against a kinsman's cock. If he does not think the cock will win, he may not bet at all, or if he is obligated by loyalties to bet but does not want to, he may simply wander off for a snack or cup of coffee.

All fights, then, are sociologically important. Often individuals who are involved in what Geertz terms "an institutionalized hostility relationship" will bet heavily against each other in what clearly is an open attack on their masculinity—the basis of status. Such hostility can come to an end if one bets on rather than against the other's cock (438–39).

While all this—animal fury, male narcissism, betting, prestige, envy and rivalry, blood sacrifice—is going on, Geertz reminds us that "*no one's status really changes*" (443). Because nothing really changes, the deep interest is finally a "deep play" in which the inner feelings and desires of men have a safe place to be expressed and experienced. Such emotions are, for Geertz, what society and individuals are constructed of. This public expression of male narcissism, with all its themes in the cockfight, connects rage and the fear of rage, and, concludes Geertz, binds them "into a set of rules which at once contain them and allows them play, builds a symbolic structure in which, over and over again, the reality of their inner affliction can be intelligibly felt" (450).

If that "inner affliction can be intelligibly felt" by the participants (the men and their cocks), can that "inner affliction" be intelligibly understood, if not explained, by the anthropologist? What is the inner affliction that fuels the esteem and prestige needs, the experience and expression of male narcissism in the feathered, ambulant penises and blood sacrifice? Why do obsessively shy and indirect men engage in rituals of exposure and symbolic castration of their cocks? Geertz claims that in the cockfight the Balinese man shapes and meets a facet of his and his society's temperament, embodied in narcissistic animality (451). What is the basis of that narcissistic rage? Freud saw a connection between money and anality. Could this gambling cockfight be a male adult expression of some preoedipal, anal-sadistic rage? But rage against whom? Geertz does not choose to answer that question. He is primarily interested in deciphering the texts of a culture "by reading over the shoulders of those to whom [the text] belongs" (452).

My purpose in exploring the Balinese sentiment in the Rangda-Barong dance and the cockfight is not simply to understand Balinese culture and sentiment. Rather, I want to present an admirable anthropological analysis and interpretation of ritual that acknowledges the presence and importance of psychological elements. Geertz, in my opinion, has done that as well as any anthropologist. He is not bound to see conflict from one narrow and inadequate point of view (such as functionalism, structuralism, or symbolism). But even Geertz's cultural point of view is somewhat selective in the scope of the text he analyzes. He does not seek to go beyond the issue of prestige (that is, beyond mentioning esteem, envy, jealousy, and rage—in other words, male narcissism) as the "driving force in the society" (436). I would think that, having noted the double entendre of *cocks*, he would say something about why men find big, strong cocks so prestigious. It has to have something to do with what cocks (in the human sense) are used for: the penetration of women. This begs the question: Do women have something to do with cockfighting (and therefore sacrifice)?

Geertz is somewhat embarrassed by questions of sex and gender. In his discussion of the Rangda-Barong dance, he omits the examples of lust in the entranced people or in Rangda. In a footnote he remarks that "[s]exual differentiation is culturally extremely played down in Bali" (417–18 n. 4). But there is not much consequence to this statement because, as he also points out, most everything social or public (with the exception of these rituals) is played down in Bali. Yet he admits that the "cockfight is unusual within Balinese culture in being a single-sex [meaning male] public activity from which the other sex [meaning female] is totally and expressly excluded" (417–18 n. 4). A group of men playing ("deep playing") with their cocks does not want women present. Why? The reason has little to do with the animality of the fights. It has to do with identification and male narcissism.

Geertz does not differentiate between animal fury (what the feathered cocks are doing) and narcissistic rage (what the men are doing with their betting or, through identification, what they want to do with their own cocks). In his effort to understand the identification of man to cock (bird), he has not fully recognized the narcissistic rage and need for revenge the cock (bird and penis) symbolizes. In psychoanalytic terms, both cocks are hypocathected, split-off parts of male narcissism, not, as Geertz suggests, simply id or animality. The linchpin of this argument is recognizing that prestige (an element of narcissism) is the main cultural motivator. This does not take anything away from the brilliance of Geertz's interpretation. Kohut's revisions of the psychoanalytic theory of narcissism, from which Geertz could have benefited, was only just becoming known outside clinical psychoanalysis when Geertz wrote his essay "Deep Play: Notes on the Balinese Cockfight" in 1972.

Narcissistic rage is a reaction to narcissistic wounds (the slights and insults embodied in the gambling, much of that the result of wife-capture, inheritance disputes, politics—political disputes are often due to kinship disputes, etc.). The point I am making is that cocks are not merely about sex, but rather the symbolic sexuality of cocks is fueled with narcissism. The cockfight, then, exhibits male narcissistic elements having to do with prestige and status, which are deeply involved with patrilineal social structure and from which women are excluded.

FIVE

Anthropology, Gender, and the Search for a Theory of Mind

STRUCTURE AND KINSHIP

I HAVE BEEN using two related concepts in this review of anthropological theories of ritual and sacrifice: social structure and kinship system. Social structure has occupied a central place in anthropological analysis. It is the foundation of social classificatory systems (e.g., plant and animal taxonomies, food/not-food taxonomies, and perhaps most importantly totemism and kinship systems). In social systems that practice sacrifice, the foundation of the social structure in which the sacrifice is embedded is the kinship system. Indeed, the kinship system is often *the* social structure. The farther away from kinship system the organizing structure of society is, the less likely is ritual blood sacrifice to be found—sacrifice with actual as opposed to symbolic blood. When the kinship system is *the* social determinant, blood rituals, such as sacrifice, circumcision, body scarification, or other mutilations are found as dominant rituals.

When Durkheim sought to analyze and interpret elementary systems of classification, he understood them as reflections of social structure. Lévi-Strauss hypothesized his deep mental structures as the foundation of social structure based on his analysis of kinship and related systems. For both Douglas and Turner, among those groups with kinship systems, rituals of transformations reflect, enhance, or resolve conflicts embedded in kinship systems and relationships.

The literally hundreds of thousands of pages of anthropological writings dedicated to the analysis of kinship systems present many different (but not limitless) structures of kinship systems. Kinship systems determine where people live, who is allied with whom, who marries whom, lineage and descent, inheritance, what cattle belong to whom, what the cattle are named, what people are named, and on and on, often creating an entire social structure based on kinship. Some of these kinship rules and customs survived in modern Western society, but in societies more formally based on kinship, the rules are elaborate and extensive.

Maintaining descent (who came from whom) in a kinship system is entirely logical, if somewhat conflictual, based on an established line of descent. In a kinship system, the line of descent can run through mothers, fathers, or combinations of both. If it runs through the mothers, the descent is called matrilineal; if through the father, patrilineal; if through both, double unilineal. In the West, our last names are passed on from our fathers. Western name descent is patrilineal in its origins, although people trace their ancestry back through both sexes. In the study of his own descent, Alex Haley determined his roots by going back to his mother, her mother, her mother's mother, her mother's mother's son (Kunta Kinte), and Kunta Kinte's father. In a kinship system, such lateral movement between genders would be improbable, even though Haley's descent is no less genetically accurate. And given the absence of writing in most kinship cultures, the possibility of determining descent past a few generations becomes increasingly difficult. However, several lineage systems may be operating in a kinship system at the same time. Among the Nuer of East Africa, a person simultaneously belongs to a minimal lineage of a man, his sons, all their sons, and all those son's sons (four generations), a minor lineage (six generations) that determines a man's place in the social world, a major lineage (eight generations), a maximal lineage (ten generations), and a clan (several maximal lineages clustered together) (Evans-Pritchard 1940, 192–248).

When people in a kinship system marry, they live either with the husband's family or with the wife's family. If they live with the father, the system is patrilocal; if with the mother, matrilocal. Sometimes there is an organized way they can live with both families, hence ambilocal. There can be matrilineal-patrilocal systems, patrilineal-matrilocal systems, patrilineal-patrilocal, etc. The important thing is that in all systems, there are established rules governing whatever is supposed to occur. While these large categories may set up the living and descent arrangements, the secondary categories create the complexities, intrigue, and conflicts within kinship systems. In the modern West, kinship extends to the nuclear family and to the nuclear families of the husband and wife, and perhaps a bit further (e.g., first and second cousins). In Western kinship systems, if women marry (at least until recently) they take the last name of their husband's father.

NANCY JAY: SACRIFICE AND PATRILINEAL DESCENT

ON THE GENDER-SPECIFICS of kinship systems and sacrifice, Nancy Jay writes that when it occurs within a patrilineal descent system, "blood sacrificial ritual can serve as evidence of patrilineal descent, and in doing so it works to constitute and maintain patrilineal descent systems" (1985, 285). This is a significant insight into the relationship between kinship systems (patriliny) and sacrifice. Jay has explored two gender-related features of sacrifice as a way of understanding the social logic of the ritual. She notes (1) the polarity of social meaning between "sacrificial purity and the pollution of childbirth;" and (2) the fact that for the most part only men may perform the sacrificial ritual (283).

Jay presents evidence for the value polarity between childbirth and sacrifice. The Aztec sacrifices to the sun god demonstrate the opposition between sacrifice and childbirth, for "only repeated sacrifice gave [the sun] new life each morning and enabled it to climb upward, but it sank to its death each evening accompanied by the spirits of women dead in childbirth" (284). Ezekiel describes the diaspora as divine retribution for a life "like the uncleanness of a woman in her impurity" (Ezek. 17:36). Sacrifice is also used to purify a woman made impure through childbirth (Lev. 12:8f). And quoting the Greek historian Moulinier, Jay notes that the Greeks believed the pollution of childbirth was what separated humans from the gods in the first place—the sacrifice being the means of establishing the reconnection. An ideological polarity appears to exist between negative childbirth and positive sacrifice. And Jay asks, "What is it about childbirth that can only be undone by sacrifice?" (1985, 284).

The sociological answer to that question is found in understanding the relation between sacrifice and the kind of family/kinship systems that have sacrifice as a central part of their social meaning and ritual life. With few exceptions, sacrifice as the central act of a society's ritual life is found predominantly in patrilineal kinship systems. Even in Jay's review of societies with matrilineal and patrilineal systems operating at the same time, only the patrilineal systems sacrifice or only patrilineal members sacrifice for the matrilineal members for patrilineal purposes. Using Turner's twin categories of abandonment and prophylaxis to describe the two foci of sacrifice, Jay concludes that in the matrilineal/patrilineal system of the Ndembu, the sacrifice abandons (destructures) matriliny and provides a prophylaxis (restructuring) of the patriliny. In the definition developed by Hubert and Mauss, matriliny is made profane, patriliny made sacred. Sacrifice "provide[s] clear evidence of jural paternity" in a way which is "as powerful, definite, and available to the senses as birth" (Jay 1985, 291).

Using the Turner model, sacrifice is a way of integrating (in the communal meal of integrative sacrifices) the patrilineal descent group, and expiating descent from women (and other similar polluting dangers). Such a process is evident within the early history of Christianity, marked by the struggle of the male patriarchy of the church to establish and maintain a male descent group (the apostolic succession of bishops and priests) through the eucharistic reenactment of the sacrifice of Christ. Moreover, from the time of Augustine, the exclusion of women from the ecclesiastical hierarchy was complete, the eucharist as sacrifice was established, and the patrilineal priesthood was made canon.

Jay's very original scholarship is important for its historical and sociological insight. She has presented evidence for the relationship between patrilineal kinship systems and sacrifice. And while most anthropologists may have recognized that only men (in kinship societies) perform sacrifices, Jay has sought to understand the sociological reason why. Anthropologists have not viewed Christian rituals the same way they view non-Western cultures and rituals. Jay has pointed out some significant similarities between them.

From the title of her essay, "Sacrifice as Remedy for Having Been Born of Woman," it is clear that Jay sees sacrifice as male compensation for being born of women and for not being women. But why does the recognition of having been born of woman lead men to believe they need to remedy this? Why would such a recognition lead to sacrifice as a ritual instrument for establishing and maintaining a male-dominated social order? Geertz has argued that intentional human activity is fueled by moods and motivations. To understand the moods and motivations that led to sacrifice is to seek access to the human mind of the sacrificer—his psychology. Jay shies away from any psychological reasons why men would choose or be compelled to perform sacrifice in the face of the power (dangerous and polluting) of women and childbirth. Like Bruno Bettleheim, Jay must certainly recognize envy as part of the psychological process, but that is as far as she goes.

ANTHROPOLOGY AND DYNAMIC PSYCHOLOGY

I BEGAN PART I with a look at structural functionalism, both social (Hubert and Mauss via Durkheim) and mental (Lévi-Strauss). Lévi-Strauss, who wished to eliminate the necessity of history and conflict altogether, seems most annoyed with sacrifice, perhaps a result of his unwillingness to provide an anthropology of conflict. The works of Douglas and more so of Turner place the symbol at the heart of ritual and sacrifice. Douglas, more in the Durkheimian camp, interprets the body of the victim as a symbol of the social body—the body politic; while Turner acknowledges that "pole" of the symbol, he rebels against a too-rigid social functionalism and adds (after Edward Sapir) the sensory, orectic, or even psychodynamic pole of the symbol. In this sense ritual is a creation of, a legitimating reflection of, and a response to social patterns and ideological structures. With Turner the review moved away from the ideological reflection and toward the orectic response. Turner includes the orectic response because the conflicts and contradictions that give rise to social dramas and their ritual processes obviously express the presence of emotional affect and intrigue. And finally, Geertz's description most clearly leaves me with the strongest sense of the nature of that affect and intrigue.

Nancy Jay provides an important contribution to a more deeply contextualized theory of sacrifice. Her insistence on the relationship between sacrifice and patriliny adds to our understanding of the gender-specific origins and cultural meanings of social conflicts, structural and kinship contradictions, and male anxiety surrounding prestige and power, which are apparent in ritual blood sacrifices.

There are other theoretical orientations within anthropology, such as the British brand of structural functionalism pioneered by Radcliff-Brown, the social anthropology of Lienhardt and Evans-Pritchard, or the German conflict and social action theories born of

Marx and Weber, who, along with Durkheim, were also instrumental in the theoretical origins of social anthropology. While important within the history of anthropology, they would not greatly affect the theories of ritual and sacrifice I have discussed. Particularly in America, the symbolic and cultural anthropological orientations, exemplified by Turner and Geertz respectively, enjoy such widespread acceptance because they are the least dogmatic. However, I would also argue that the teeth of a Marxist analysis of ritual or the pessimism of Weber's view of religion are not lost to someone like Geertz. Yet, as I have noted, Geertz was unable to discuss the social reality of sexism in the cultures he studied.

If I may borrow a model from Turner, theories, like rituals, seem to be situated along a dialectical continuum between an ideological pole (Marx and the search for false consciousness) and a sensory pole of interpretation (Freud and the search for the unconscious). In my review of these twentieth-century anthropological theories, I have included those that are important to the development of an understanding of ritual and sacrifice. I have also chosen orientations that occupy different locations on the theory continuum. And I have chosen ones that recognize and try to respond to the obvious psychological elements of ritual. But the most important reason I have chosen these and not others is because they ask the questions I want to answer: questions of identification, sentiment or affection, as well as those of power, prestige, and conflict. Answers to these questions require a more systematic developmental and dynamic model of the mind. In Part II I explore some of these models.

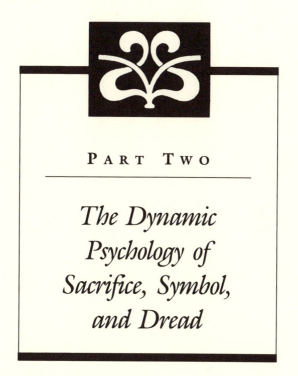

PART TWO

*The Dynamic
Psychology of
Sacrifice, Symbol,
and Dread*

S I X

Sigmund Freud:
Sacrifice, Symbols, and the Uncanny

I think I would have raised an outcry if I had believed my eyes. But, I didn't believe them at first—
the thing seems so impossible. The fact is I was
completely unnerved by a sheer blank fright, a pure
abstract terror, unconnected with any distinct shape
of physical danger. What made this emotion so over-
powering was—how shall I define it?—the moral
shock I received, as if something altogether monstrous, intolerable to thought and odious to the soul
had been thrust upon me unexpectedly.

Joseph Conrad, *Heart of Darkness*

OEDIPAL ANXIETY AND SACRIFICE

FREUD CLAIMS THAT the "beginnings of religion, ethics, society, and
art converge in the Oedipus Complex" (1913, 156). Drawing on the
work of W. Robertson Smith, he argues that sacrifice "plays the same
role in all religion, so that its origins must be traced back to very
general causes, operating everywhere in the same manner" (133). Religious sacrifice, no matter how that ritual had been transformed
through the history of a culture, represents a symbolic reenactment
of the Oedipus complex, which has its prehistoric origins in acts of
patricide and incest. Such an argument makes three key assumptions:
(1) The plausibility of prehistoric acts assumes a social order along
the lines of Darwin's primal horde. (2) The symbolic reenactment of

67

the act assumes the existence of an unconscious genetic memory of the original act. (3) The reenactment depends on the psychodynamic tension between desire and repulsion (i.e., ambivalence) for its unconscious motivation.

Freud's effort to base a theory of sacrifice on the genetic inheritance of a racial memory is notably unpsychoanalytic. His theory of sacrifice need not and cannot rest on such a Lamarckian chimera. Likewise, the assumption that prehistoric hordes of men behaved in the manner proposed by Darwin is more fantasy than fact. His analysis of ambivalence, anxiety, and symptom-formation, however, could be helpful in psychoanalytically explaining sacrifice. In this chapter I begin with Freud's explicit theory of sacrifice and then examine other parts of Freud's theory to understand the ritual in a deeper psychoanalytic context. To begin, Freud describes the sacrificial victim as a patricidal substitute: "The totem animal is in reality a substitute for the father; and this tallies with the contradictory fact that, though the killing of the animal is as a rule forbidden, yet its killing is a festive occasion—with the fact that it is killed yet mourned. The ambivalent emotional attitude, which to this day characterizes the father-complex in our children and which often persists into adult life, seems to extend to the totem animal in its capacity as substitute for the father" (141).

This "ambivalent attitude" is the psychodynamic conflict between desire for and repulsion of the mother, and between the idealization of and fear of the father. It is also the source of anxiety—the ego's reaction to instinctual and external dangers. The instinctual demand of the id for the mother is dangerous because of the external threat of castration, death, or other object loss from the father. The external danger is introjected as part of the superego. While the id demands satisfaction, the superego demands punishment. Both demands are deflected by and onto the ego and form the origins of ambivalence and anxiety.

The ego guards against anxiety by repressing the instinctual demands of the id. But, as Freud so often points out, the repression of the drives is never absolute; the original aims are never eliminated. More often the ego is successful in transforming the aims into other behavioral forms or symptomatic repressions. Such symptom-formation is comprised of two aspects: "One, hidden from view, brings about the alteration of the id in virtue of which the ego is removed from danger; the other, presented more openly, shows what has been created in place of the instinctual process that has been effected—namely the substitutive formation" (1926, 145). This explanation of the origins of symptom-formation shows some affinity with the definition of sacrifice of Hubert and Mauss, of which Freud was aware. Transforming the danger, the symptom functions as a precaution, an expiation, or a prohibition. But it also functions as a substitutive satisfaction. Thus the symptom, like sacrifice, is or can be both conjunctive and disjunctive. Conjunctive sacrifices attempt to obtain closer contact with the divine power; disjunctive sacrifices seek a separation or distance from that power. Freud argued a similar line in his theory of symptom-formation. Yet, while it may be ideologically clear what the man wants in a sacrifice, the psychological structures behind that ideology remain hidden. Freud sought an explanation of sacrifice as being analogous to obsessional neuroses. The neurotic symptom is triumphant "if it succeeds in combining the prohibition with the satisfaction" (112). What appears as ambivalence (desire and repulsion) in anxiety, appears as ambiguity (satisfaction and prohibition) in the symptom.

Because Freud considered neurotic symptom-formation analogous to symbolic rituals, he understood sacrifice to be the public expression of repressed wishes and prohibitions of the Oedipus complex. The incestuous desire of the son(s) is inhibited by the fear of a powerful father who is subsequently hated by the son. Such hatred leads to the desire to commit patricide. In sacrifice the victim symbolically represents the father. The affect surrounding the symbolic patricide is ambivalence. While being hated, the father is also idealized by the son. Because of this idealization, the patricide creates a sense of guilt, with an increased reverence for the father and a renunciation of the object of incestuous desire. Freud's oedipal theory of sacrifice has been supported without any appreciable theoretical change by both Roger Money-Kyrle (1930) and Theodor Reik (1930, 1957).

In a recent study of the psychology of sacrifice, René Girard (1977, 169–92) notes that Freud's Oedipus complex contains a very strong mimetic element, which Freud suppressed. He argues that Freud's understanding of the process of identification anticipates and resembles the idea of mimetic desire. Freud writes: "A little boy will exhibit a special interest in his father; he would like to be like him, and take his place everywhere. We may simply say that he takes his father as his ideal. This behavior has nothing to do with a passive or feminine attitude toward his father (and towards males in general); it is, on the contrary, typically masculine. It fits in very well with the Oedipus complex, for which it helps prepare the way" (1921, 105). This passage suggests that the desire to be like the father precedes and leads to the incestuous desire for the mother. Girard points out that the incestuous desire could in fact be a desire to imitate the idealized father. In a later work, however, Freud contends that the sexual cathexis of the mother is an autonomous and more primal desire. In his failure to maintain the mimetic quality of the Oedipus complex, Freud, claims Girard, has to assume a level of awareness for the ego, which is more likely to be found in adults. Girard suggests that the son desires the mother because the father desires her.

A satisfactory Freudian theory of sacrifice is not to be found in *Totem and Taboo*, where almost everyone now finds Freud's theory to be inadequate. It is unsatisfactory not only from an anthropological point of view, where Freud has been criticized the most, but also from a psychoanalytic point of view. From the more important psychoanalytic point of view, the error Freud made was in his theory of anxiety. Unable to appreciate anxiety as anything other than separation anxiety, Freud could not see that another class of anxiety, distinct from that of the threat of object loss, was possible. For Freud, the *loss* of merger with the mother gives rise to anxiety (1926, 138). The possibility of a regressive merger itself could not, in Freud's opinion, activate a non-separation, non-oedipal anxiety. This confusion is further compounded by the analysand's use of separation themes in describing the fear of regressive merger (or other narcissistic anxieties). Nevertheless, while Freud was unable to recognize any specific theoretical connection between narcissistic anxiety and sacrifice, he did recognize some connection between oedipal anxiety and narcissism.

As previously noted, the id's desire is perceived by the ego as dangerous, and anxiety is the ego's reaction to such danger. While Freud sought to place the Oedipus complex at the center of his psychoanalytic psychology, he recognized that the fear of castration was but one of several examples of anxiety involving the danger of losing a love object. An earlier example is the anxiety "conditioned by separation from the mother" (138). The fear of castration is one form of the fear of separation: the fear of separation from one's genitals. The penis possesses a special narcissistic value because, according to Freud, it is the organ by which the id can merge with the original lost object (the mother), thus restoring the original sense of undifferentiated unity (primary narcissism). Geertz's study of cockfighting exemplifies this narcissistic value of the penis (cock). But Geertz's study points to qualities of narcissism that are not solely expressive of oedipal themes. For this reason the conflicts of the Balinese (or the Lele or the Ndembu) cannot be sufficiently explained using an oedipal typology. This is not to say that sexual themes and male identity are not operating in a great many of these rituals—but it is clear that the conflict between a father and a son are not at the root of these rituals. However, the same may not be said of a conflict between a man and a woman (or between a father and the mother of his children). Such a conflict does not revolve around gender identity but gender identification. Freud was aware of this, but, as with his seduction theory, he could not place the origins of the conflicts (oedipal, gender, or generational) in the psychic apparatus of male preoedipal narcissism (including that hypocathected onto the penis and mistaken as the Oedipus complex by Freud).

Although Freud indicated a progression from the loss of the mother to castration to moral (social) anxiety, he only indirectly developed the relationship between anxiety and non- or preoedipal narcissism. Nor did he develop the relationship between narcissism and sacrifice. In *Totem and Taboo* Freud notes that animism (the forerunner of totemism and religion) represents the unconscious belief in the "omnipotence of thought." Omnipotent thought is characteristic of the narcissistic period of development between autoeroticism and true object love. But Freud's focus on the Oedipus complex kept him from seeing the role of narcissism itself in sacrifice. Elsewhere in Freud's writings are elements for a theoretical bridge between narcissism and sacrifice. His work on narcissism, sublimation, and even the uncanny are such places to look. But these must be examined within the context of a larger theory of symbolization and symbol formation because the developmental and the ritual converge in the symbol.

SYMBOLIZATION, SUBLIMATION, AND NARCISSISM

FREUD PROVIDES SIGNIFICANT insight into the psychological relation between culture and symbol. Although not its only function, culture is the origin of normative thought and behavior, embodied in parents and introjected as the superego. The superego is the psychological repository of cultural artifacts. These internalized artifacts repress libidinal aims and force the ego through several types of defenses (e.g., repression, reaction-formation, sublimation) to channel the aims onto internal psychic structures, transitional somatic symptoms, or external, desexualized objects. Culture is usually seen by Freud as the coercive antithesis of libidinal aims. What culture renounces, the superego represses.

But the symbols of culture can also be the means of satisfying what culture (through the parents and superego) renounces. Freud's interest in symbolization began with the psychological meaning of dreams. Here, as with symptom-formation, the occurrence of symbols results from the anxiety and ambivalence surrounding a desire and its prohibition. In a dream a symbol represents a disguised desire and its gratification, which the ego provides in place of the original object. But Freud was more concerned with how symbols function in dreams (i.e., condensation, displacement, and representation) than with how symbolization is possible in the first place.

An obvious question to ask, however, is, Where do these symbols and their meaning come from and how do they get into the psychological apparatus in the first place? Freud replies that "we learn it from very different sources—from fairy tales and myths, from buffoonery and jokes, from folklore (that is, from knowledge about popular manners and customs, sayings and songs) and from poetic and colloquial linguistic usage" (1916–17, 158–59). Commenting on this passage, Paul Ricoeur notes that "it is not the dream work that constructs the symbolic relation, but the work of culture" (1970, 500 n. 10). Freud seems to be saying that the moral artifacts that comprise the superego and the symbols of the dream are both introjected products of culture. The symbol represents the object and the aim of the drive; the superego provides the means and necessity of expressing the drive in symbolic form. In other words, the symbol and the superego are somehow part of the same process, the process of sublimation, combining the ethical qualities of the superego with the aesthetic qualities of the sublimated aim (the sublime). Ricoeur claims that Freud's use of sublimation creates more problems than it resolves because it remains too imprecise, a point made earlier by Norman Brown (1959, 137–44). Yet what is this process of sublimation?

Sublimation relates the individual psychological apparatus to society and culture. Sublimation is the cultural imposition of repression *and* at the same time, "sublimation is a way out, a way by which those demands of the ego can be met *without* involving repression" (Freud 1914, 95; *see also* 1923, 28–47). Both Ricoeur and Brown complain that this contradictory definition of sublimation confuses the issue more than it clarifies. I suggest that we can understand the apparent contradictions in Freud's inchoate theory of sublimation by seeing it as part of an evolving psychology of narcissism. Sublimation accomplishes a redirection of desexualized aim by changing object libido into narcissistic libido. The object of libidinal aim is decathected from the object and recathected onto the ego. "The character of the ego is a precipitate of abandoned object-cathexes" (1923, 36). Sublimation thus can be both a renunciation and an expression (unconscious perhaps) of the higher, subliminal aim. Moreover, the process of sublimation is not so much an abandonment of object-cathexes as it is a search for a now-idealized narcissistic object (the sublime). Without fully understanding the role of narcissism in sublimation, nevertheless, Brown correctly defines sublimation as "a search in the outside world for the lost body of childhood" (1959, 289). In other words, sublimation, like melancholia (another aspect of Freud's theory of narcissism), represents the ego's effort to psychologically mourn the loss of the object.

Ricoeur is unhappy with Freud's lack of specificity with regard to the process of sublimation in relation to both desexualization and introjection (or identification). How is object libido transformed into narcissistic libido? How is the libido desexualized? The original objects involved in the process of identification are certainly internalized as the superego. But they are the libidinal objects as well. The superego is as much a part of the id as it is of the internalized objects themselves. Freud accounts for this conceptual discrepancy by assuming that sublimation (and by extension symbolization) is a regressive process from an object relation to a narcissistic one, from a sexual one to a desexualized one. To do this, Freud proposes a dual function of identification: the desire to have (a function of object libido) and the desire to be like (a function of narcissistic libido). By first identifying with the object, internalizing it, and then sublimating it (symbolically expressing it), the psychological apparatus moves from the dangerous aims of object libido to narcissism. Through identification and sublimation, the lost or forbidden object is introjected and expressed. Both Ricoeur and Brown, however, reject the idea that all symbolization is a regression to narcissism (as Freud defines it). In addition, Ricoeur correctly sees that both identification and sublimation are not very conducive to incorporation into Freud's drive theory. He notes Freud's own dissatisfaction: "I myself am far from satisfied with these remarks on identification; but it will be enough if you can grant me that the installation of the superego can be described as a successful instance of identification with the parental agency" (Freud 1933, 63; quoted in Ricoeur 1970, 481 n. 17). Ricoeur's solution to this dilemma is to propose not only a regressive function of symbols (what he terms the symbol's archeology), but a progressive, prophetic, or teleological function of the symbol as well. It is this non-repressive aspect of sublimation that leads to the conclusion that sublimation is symbolization: "Sublimation is not a supplementary procedure that could be accounted for by an economics of desire. It is not a mechanism that could be put on the same plane as the other instinctual vicissitudes, alongside reversal, turning around upon the self, and repression. Insofar as revealing and disguising coincide in it, we might say that sublimation is the symbolic function itself" (Ricoeur 1970, 497).

Whether Ricoeur succeeds in this project is another matter, one that is beyond the scope of this book. His own struggle with Freud's ideas about sublimation, identification, and their relation to narcissism is, I believe, a genuine reflection of Freud's own struggle to incorporate these three ideas into an ego psychology. They do not quite fit. It is interesting to note, however, that Ricoeur did not choose to pursue these ideas through the history of psychoanalysis where sublimation becomes less and less important or through his (Ricoeur's) subsequent work. If we recognize, as I suggested above, that sublimation is a process of narcissism rather than of the object libido, then the ideas of identification, internalization, and symbolization remain central to theories of object relations, the self, as well as to culture and religion.

The shortcoming of Freud's theory of object relations stems from his reluctance to include social reality and cultural participation as structural elements of his metapsychology. "He did not," writes Winnicott, "get so far as to tell us where in the mind cultural experience is" (1971a, 95). The systemic basis for behavior is not simply the product of drives, nor is it the sublimated expression of those drives. Identification is not merely transformed instincts. Identification is the means by which external reality (be that first a mother, a father, the family, or society itself) acquires psychological internal structure. While he struggles and fails to maintain a psychobiological basis for identification, Freud does point to the means of such object relational acquisition when he writes that the "ego wishes to incorporate this object into itself, and in accordance with the oral or cannibalistic phase of libido development in which it is, it wants to do so by devouring it" (1917, 249–50). Understanding how that happens will help us understand the relationship between men, women, and sacrifice.

SYMBOLS, THE UNCANNY, AND THE FEAR OF WOMEN

THE PREOEDIPAL DEVOURING (introjection) of the breast was not sufficiently explored by Freud. In particular, he makes no structural connection between preoedipal devouring and the disdain by men for women based on the male fear of being castrated or devoured by women. Freud was, however, very interested in how attitudes toward women developed in the individual man. Such attitudes are evident, for example, in the taboo of virginity. Freud argued that a "generalized dread of women" is expressed in all rules concerning the avoidance of women. "Perhaps this dread is based on the fact that woman is different from man, forever incomprehensible and mysterious, strange and therefore apparently hostile. The man is afraid of being weakened by the woman, infected with her femininity, and of then showing himself incapable [of an erection?]" (1918, 249–50). The origin of such dread is located within the castration fear of the Oedipus complex. At some point in early development, the male infant becomes aware of the sexual dissimilarities between himself and his mother; that is, primary narcissism gives way to narcissism of small distinctions. Thus, the disdain and fear of women stems from the mother's lack of a penis. Freud believed he found the reason underlying "the narcissistic rejection of women by men, which is so much mixed up with despising them, drawing attention to the castration complex and its influence on the opinion in which women are held" (199). Freud's recognition of the universally found taboos by men of women, the origins of which were first explored in *Totem and Taboo*, was based to a large extent on his analysis of men and women. Men fantasize that women want to castrate and devour (incorporate) their penises. This is understood in direct relationship to female fantasies of enmity and penis envy. Freud concludes that "such a danger really exists, so that with the taboo of virginity primitive [and modern] man is defending himself against a correctly sensed, although psychical, danger" (201). Freud has been challenged on this conclusion. Penis envy is as much a fantasy of men about women. And, as women have pointed out, it is not the penis they want, but the social liberty that comes with the possession of the organ. Interestingly, on Malekula, men who are the ones who sacrifice to the devouring spirit Le-hev-hev wear elaborate penis wrappers, which are checked over carefully before the pigs are sacrificed. Like Freud, perhaps the men of Malekula fear that the devouring mother-woman wants their penises.

Freud argues for the primary relationship among these fears, intuitions, and fantasies and instincts. He states that "an instinct appears . . . on the frontier between the mental and the somatic" (1915a, 121–22). But it is also characterized as an "urge inherent in organic life to return to an earlier state of things" (1920, 43). An instinct is both a psychic representation of urges or stimuli coming from within the physical organism and effecting the mind *and* it represents the limitations and expectations of the mind made upon the physical organism. Freud distinguishes two types of instincts: the self-preservation or ego instincts and the sexual instincts. He later adds the death instinct (an aspect of narcissism as problematic as the other aspects of narcissism). Because instincts are unconscious they can in fact only be represented by ideas, and even if the idea is found in the unconscious, it is itself not the instinct.

Does Freud's drive theory suggest an instinctual basis for what has been termed "the cannibalistic, castrating mother of fantasy"? (Ducey 1976, 196). Freud understands unconscious fantasy in terms similar to those of instincts. In early correspondences with Fliess, Freud understood fantasies as psychical structures acting as barriers between the instinctual ideas and consciousness. The purpose of the repressive unconscious fantasy is to keep the instinctual representation from becoming conscious. While the instinct is the ideational representation, the psychical structure of fantasy is understood in some sense as an impulse. (For the instinct as representative of impulse, *see* Freud 1915b, 177; for the structure of fantasy as impulse, *see* Freud 1911, 222.) In spite of the apparent structural parallel of instinct and fantasy and their intimate connection, however, as far as

I can tell, Freud never actually equates them. Nevertheless, there could be a connection between the sexual stages of development and the devouring mother fantasy. I have found several places where Freud indicates such a connection.

During the analysis of some patients, Freud came across fantasies he termed oral-sadistic and anal-sadistic (aggressive). Sometimes Freud assumes that such aggressiveness results from the regressive fear of being killed by the mother. Such fear, therefore, "justifies" the death-wish against the mother (1931, 132). The infant appears to want to destroy the mother who provides nourishment because the infant fears the mother. Freud goes on to suggest that toilet training might be a causal factor in the primal fear and the sadistic regression. At other times the negative mother image in infantile fantasies is understood as fear of the phallic mother, in which the breast represents the penis and the power to destroy (1919a, 189). In both cases the fantasies are of a castrational (oedipal) character stemming from sex differentiation and the incest taboo.

Because Freud assumes a biological innateness to fantasy patterns, an interpretation of the symbol of the devouring mother based on the Oedipus complex would have to be cross-culturally demonstrable. In India for example, "the Indian fantasy life is to a great extent organized around [the] image of an angry, incorporative, fickle mother, against whom anger is directed and from whom, through a process of projection, counter aggression is feared" (Nandy 1976, 306). In Freud's theory, fear gives rise to both the image of the phallic mother and infantile aggression, and the fear is that of castration. In Nandy's account it is a more generalized fear that "women will betray, aggress, pollute, or at least fail to protect" (307). Another native of India, the psychoanalyst Kakar, confirms Nandy's view, but, unlike Freud, assumes that the fantasy of the angry mother is based on non-regressed oral fantasies, not oedipal fantasies. In a description of the healer, Baba, such fantasies of the devouring mother in India correspond to those described by Klein (Kakar 1982, 28). The Kleinian theory was known to Freud, but rejected because he did not believe that the "prehistoric," preoedipal stage could be as symbolic as Klein assumes (*see* chapter 8). In a recent psychoanalytic study of male rites in Papua New Guinea, Lidz and Lidz (1989) propose that the dread of menstrual blood stems not from a castration projection but from the smell of the mother during menstruation. In this theory the mother's non-menstrual odor enhances a sense of security and attachment, which menstrual odor disrupts. Lidz and Lidz seem less clear about why it is that men retain the disgust and dread while women do not.

If symbolization is a result of sublimation, and sublimation is the regressive transformation of object libido into narcissistic libido, then somehow the symbolization of the dread of women must be related to narcissism. As noted above, the disdain for women is "a narcissistic rejection of women by men" because men fear women, and this narcissistic fear of women has to do with differences as much as with castration anxiety.

In one essay, Freud's analysis of the uncanny sheds light on the narcissistic dread of women. He begins by defining the uncanny as "that class of the frightening which leads back to what is known of old and long familiar" (1919b, 220). To understand the uncanny is to discover the psychological apparatus that changes the once known into the dreaded. As we would expect, Freud concludes that the now unknown (in German, *unheimlich*, meaning unhomely) and dreaded is the object of incestuous desire and castration dread. Yet, there are other experiences of the uncanny. One such experience is expressed in the theme of the "double," which is an assurance against extinction. While Freud claims that the doubling (or multiplying) of genital symbols in dreams is an expression of the overcoming of castration fear, he also claims that "such ideas [of the double] . . . have sprung from the soil of unbounded self-love, from the primary narcissism which dominates the mind of the child and of primitive man. But when this stage has been surmounted the 'double' reverses its aspects. From having been an assurance of immortality, it becomes the uncanny harbinger of death" (235). Freud then reasons that the psychological process leading to a double, which starts out as the preserver and becomes the destroyer, is the same process that produces the superego. This narcissistic double treats the ego like an object. Freud further claims that the psychological propensity to double is an example of repetition-compulsion.

The experience of the uncanny can also have a related quality of "omnipotence of thoughts" (240). Evil thoughts, projected envy, magical powers, animism, witchcraft, and more are the content of a psychological process whereby thinking or imagining can become an act that is powerful, harmful, and frightening. Freud considers these to be further examples of uncontained narcissism. These qualities then—animism, magic and witchcraft, the omnipotence of thought, man's attitude to death, involuntary repetition, and the castration complex—make up the experience of the uncanny. Freud concludes by suggesting how the uncanny arises: "An uncanny effect is often and easily produced when the distinction between imagination and reality is effaced, as when something that we have hitherto regarded as imaginary appears before us in reality, or when a symbol takes over the full functions of the thing it symbolizes" (244). The experience of the uncanny occurs in the psychological margin between image and reality, where the distinctions or the boundaries between the image (symbol) and the real are blurred, where the subjective image psychologically merges with objective reality.

This definition of the uncanny could very well function as a definition of certain aspects of narcissism. In reading "The Uncanny," I was struck by the uncanny way that Freud's analysis of the uncanny leads him to the dread of women. For in attempting to define the uncanny, Freud looks at the word *unheimlich* (unhomely) and realizes what "the home" really is. He remarks that "it often happens that neurotic men declare that they feel there is something uncanny about the female genital organs. This *unheimlich* place, however, is the entrance to the former *Heim* [home] of all human beings, to the place where each one of us lived once upon a time and in the beginning" (245).

Thus Freud argues for two sources of the experience of the uncanny: a narcissistic source (represented by omnipotence of thoughts) and a return of the repressed libidinal source (represented by the castration complex or womb fantasies). Freud attempts to explain what appear both as separate sources of experiences of the uncanny (narcissistic libido and object libido) and as related elements: "When we consider that primitive beliefs [narcissism] are most intimately connected with infantile complexes [object libido], and are, in fact, based upon them, we shall not be greatly astonished to find that the distinction is often a hazy one" (249).

This remark points up the contradictory nature of Freud's effort to incorporate narcissism into his drive theory. The problem is that the stage of primary narcissism precedes object choice and libidinal cathexes. Yet Freud cannot grant the narcissistic stage any symbolizing ability, so psychologically primitive beliefs (narcissism) are based on a later developmental stage. Freud cannot yield on this. Images of the dreaded, uncanny mother are not representative of a preoedipal, narcissistic period. Although regression to such a period is possible, the images and fantasies in such a regression remain oedipal. Freud could not accept the possibility that the converse might be true, that the castration complex was an eroticized example of a deeper, narcissistic anxiety.

In his psychoanalytic study of ritual genital mutilation among Australian aborigines, Bettelheim (1955) argued that the dread of women reflects an envy of their procreative capacities. This envy expresses the ambivalence boys (and girls) have about their own gender identity, which originates in the pregenital experience with the mother and lasts anywhere from seven to fifteen years. Expanding this theory, Lidz and Lidz argue that there are many preoedipal influences affecting a boy's male identity. They put the emphasis on "the boy's need to rescind his identification with his mother and not simply on how the erotic [oedipal] aspect of his love for her and attachment to her is resolved or repressed" (1989, 178).

Having argued for a relation among narcissism, symbolization, and the dread of women, the next step is to relate these to the symbolic ritual of sacrifice. Freud's metapsychology does not permit this. His inability to place the mother-child experience within his theory is the chief reason why a theory of women and sacrifice cannot rely solely on Freud for its psychology, although the seeds of such a theory have clearly been sown by Freud.

Seven

Carl Jung: Introversion, Sacrifice, and the Mother

Except as part of the history of psychoanalysis, the theories of Carl Jung are rarely used in psychoanalytic literature. This is unfortunate for two reasons. First, psychoanalysis shows an obvious and pervasive resistance to proposing a psychoanalytic theory of culture. Jung shared no such reluctance, and, although his efforts are sometimes less than satisfactory, his belief that introversion leads to cultural change is not really as strange as his detractors might believe. Second, Jung's contribution within the context of the psychoanalytic movement was much more substantial than psychoanalytic historians had wanted to believe (Homans 1979). For these two reasons, I have included a short chapter on Jung.

INTROVERSION AND SACRIFICE

In the same year Freud published his theory of sacrifice in *Totem and Taboo*, Jung published *Wadungen und Symbole der Libido*, which in English became *Symbols of Transformation* (1967). In this book he presented a theory of sacrifice significantly different from that of Freud. According to Jung, sacrifice symbolically reflects a confrontation with and renunciation of the desire to return to the womb. Such renunciation does not come from castration fear, as in Freud's theory, but from the desire to be free from the original state of unconsciousness within the primal or archetypal mother, which is prior to the individual experience of the human mother.

81

Symbols of Transformation is a highly problematic book. Peter Homans has argued that Jung's deteriorating relationship with Freud played a significant role in the writing of the book (1979, 60–73). Nevertheless, intellectually their conflict was about the libido theory. In *Symbols of Transformation* the libido theory, upon which Freud based both the Oedipus complex and sacrifice, was directly challenged by Jung. The heart of the challenge was that the fear of incest is not transformed into castration fear but rather fear of "being devoured by the mother" (Jung 1967, 419). Libidinal regression to sexual incest is only an allegorical regression. The psychic motivation for incest has to do with a presexual lure to a state of unconsciousness in the mother's womb.

In this theory Jung recognized the symbolic significance of margins and borderlines (the liminal period of ritual) within the context of sacrifice. For example, in his analysis of Longfellow's poem, "The Song of Hiawatha," Jung notes that the first act of the hero, Hiawatha, is to kill a roebuck by a ford in a river:

> Then upon one knee uprising,
> Hiawatha aimed an arrow;
> Scarce a twig moved with his motion,
> Scarce a leaf was stirred or rustled,
> But the wary roebuck startled,
> Stamped with all his hoofs together,
> Listened with one foot uplifted,
> Leaped as if to meet the arrow;
> Ah! The singing fatal arrow,
> Like a wasp it buzzed and stung him!
>   Dead he lay there in the forest,
> By the ford across the river;
> Beat his timid heart no longer. (Longfellow, 139)

Jung understood this scene as "the borderline between the conscious [land] and the unconscious [water, amniotic fluid]" (1967, 327). Because animals are a part of nature ("Mother Nature"), to kill one is to somehow overcome and possess some of the immense power of the mother, i.e., the unconscious. Jung considered the unconscious to be the maternal matrix out of which develops the conscious. The unconscious can be overcome and its power appropriated only through contact with it at the margin of the conscious and the unconscious. By crossing the river the hero achieves the critical degree of con-

sciousness necessary to confront and assimilate the power of the unconscious (symbolized by the killing of the roebuck) and moves "out
of childhood into manhood" (Longfellow, 140). (An interesting aside
to the roebuck, which might have bothered Jung and would have
pleased Freud: the male roebuck has been observed killing and eating
immature roebucks.)

In addition to marginality, Jung also recognized a danger in
not "fording the stream of unconsciousness" (1967, 326) The unconscious is comprised of both the personal unconscious and the instinctual, autonomous archetypes of the collective unconscious. It is
the archetypes that represent the chief danger in the maturational
process:

> The libido that will flow into life at the right times regresses to
> the mythical world of the archetypes, where it activates images
> which since the remotest times have expressed the non-human
> life of the Gods, whether of the upper or the lower. If this
> regression occurs in a young person, his own individual life is
> supplanted by the divine archetypal drama, which is all the more
> devastating for him because his conscious education provides
> him with no means of recognizing what is happening, and thus
> with no possibility of freeing him from its fascination. (309)

In freeing himself from the dangerous fascination and luring power
of the archetypal unconscious (through the process of individuation),
the hero sacrifices his mother-libido (the union of mother and child).
The success of the sacrifice can only occur on the borderline of the
conscious and the unconscious in the process of introversion.

The developing psyche's efforts to free itself from the illusion
of undifferentiated experience occurs as the constellated archetypes
are confronted and overcome. The danger of such a confrontation
lies in the enthralling, mnemonic power of undifferentiated psychological experience (total merger of self and object) at the breast or
in the womb. In the transformation of the epigenetic necessity and
danger in the psyche to the public expression of the same process in
myth and ritual, most sacrifices serve as the violent meeting ground
of both regressive and developmental tendencies:

> The impulse to sacrifice proceeds . . . from the *mater saeva cu-*
> *pidium* [savage mother of desire]. . . . As a primal being the
> mother represents the unconscious; hence, the myth tells us that

the impulse to sacrifice comes from the unconscious. This is to be understood in the sense that regression is inimical to life and disrupts the instinctual foundations of personality, and is consequently followed by the compensatory reaction taking the form of violent suppression and elimination of the incompatible tendency. It is a natural, unconscious process, a collision between instinctive tendencies. (424)

Jung's *Symbols of Transformation* lacks cohesion and ethnographic application. It is, according to Homans, "a record of Jung's own fantasies, not an interpretation of the myths and symbols of the past" (1979, 66). Like Freud, Jung seems to have developed much of his psychodynamic theory from his own self-analysis. But using ethnography and mythology as bulwarks of that theory brings Jung no closer to understanding what he discovered than it did Freud. This is not to say that the theory is not useful to us. On the contrary, to say that a person's creative and intellectual endeavors are formed and fueled by personal history and struggle does not invalidate that endeavor. In spite of their obvious theoretical shortcomings, I appreciate Jung and Freud as explorers into both their own and all *male* psyches. While Jung's theory of sacrifice lacks some degree of credibility, as with Freud, his work on symbol formation is important in seeing the relationship between the developing child and its mother. A more accurate Jungian theory of symbolic sacrifice lies in understanding the developmental relation among mother, infant, and symbol formation.

ARCHETYPES OF THE MOTHER UNCONSCIOUS

FOR BOTH HISTORICAL and personal reasons, Jung picked up the themes of religion, sublimation (what he termed *introversion*), symbols, and the psyche. As a physician, Jung's focus continued to be the individual, but his emphasis on the primacy of the individual is not as crucial as it was for Freud. His analysis of the individual, indeed the very method of Jungian psychology, begins with society. Thus he understands society as both the expression of individual human potential and the sociocultural necessity for human development. Jung has a specific understanding of the social. The social is the unconscious, more specifically, the collective unconscious. Consciousness is the small part of the psyche having to do with the ego. Consciousness, the ego, and individuality come into being as part of the individuation process. But it is the self emerging out of the individuation process that becomes the center of the psyche. As noted above, the collective unconscious, out of which the self as well as the ego and consciousness emerge, is comprised of undifferentiated symbols called archetypes. The archetypes appear to the individual as a kind of dream scene or repository of dream images. The archetypes appear to society as collective representations. But these archetypes can only be expressed in particular manifestations by individuals. The archetype "must individuate itself," writes Jung, "as soon as it manifests itself, for there is no way in which it can express itself except through the single individual" (1939, 296). Each personal psyche differentiates or individuates out of the collective representations comprised of the archetypes. "The crux of the matter is that the archetypes of the collective experience, which are the symbols of society, must be expressed through individuals; on the other hand, individuals must rely on collective material for the basic content of their personality" (Progoff 1973, 153).

The movement between the individual and the collective is termed "psychic energy," and Jung argues that this psychic energy can be transformed as it creates both individual and culture (including ritual) in the tension between both. To understand ritual sacrifice, then, is first to understand the relation among the archetypes, psychic energy, and symbol formation. In Jung's theory of the origins of symbol formation, archetypes play an essential role. Archetypes are the biologically inherited patterns of thought and behavior that comprise the collective unconscious. They are the pre-existent unconscious images of instincts, which are distinctive to the whole (collective) species. During the life cycle of an individual, various internal and environmental conditions help constellate these archetypes. The collective unconscious is a phylogenetic structure with an epigenetic function. The epigenetic actuation of the archetypes is what Jung terms the process of individuation.

Through much of his work we can find Jung's tireless effort to indicate the necessary relation between individual dreams and fantasies and cultural myths and symbols. By analyzing these symbolic representations, the archetypal patterns can be illuminated by the depth psychologist with the help of the anthropologist and historian. While these archetypal patterns are as multivariable as their symbolic representations, their functional qualities are controlled by natural limits. This has implications not only for symbol formation but also for personal and cultural activity. "Although the changing situations of life must appear infinitely various to our way of thinking, their possible number never exceeds certain natural limits; they fall into more or less typical patterns that repeat themselves over and over again" (Jung 1967, 294). Interestingly, Lévi-Strauss does not acknowledge the similarity between his idea of deep structural mythemes and Jung's idea of the archetypes, although such similarity is obvious: "If we add that these structures [mythemes] are not only the same for everyone and for all areas to which the function applies," writes Lévi-Strauss, "but that they are very few in number, we shall understand why the world of symbolism is infinitely varied in content, but always limited in its laws" (1967, 199). Archetypes are genetically determined and limited and developmentally determining and limiting. Symbol formation cannot be understood apart from its relation to inherited instincts, because symbols derive their motive power from the instinctually determined archetypes.

The analysis of dreams, fantasies, the active imagination of patients, and the symbols of cultural myths gives a fairly large catalog of representations of the archetypes. Among the most important in Jung's system is the Archetypal Feminine. The Archetypal Feminine represents an extensive potential of archetypal aspects, one of which is the Mother archetype. As in the case of all archetypes, the Mother archetype consists of positive and negative aspects. The negative aspect is the archetype of the "Terrible Mother." It connotes anything "secret, hidden, dark; the abyss, the world of the dead, anything that devours, seduces, and poisons, that is terrifying and inescapable like fate" (Jung 1959, 82). In various cultures a symbolic representation of the Terrible Mother is the whale-dragon with "jaws of death in which men are crunched and ground to pieces" (1967, 251). At other times it is seen as a threatening serpent that seeks to devour men. The devouring aspect of the symbolic representation of the archetype is closely connected with that of entwining and embracing. According to Jung, the embracing/devouring monster/dragon/serpent represents the unconscious dread of the mother's womb. To re-enter the womb would be to extinguish consciousness and thus to die. This relationship between the mother and death is suggested in the Egyptian hieroglyph for *mother* (*Mu*), which is a vulture—a bird that feeds on the flesh of dead animals. The Terrible Mother is, like all archetypes, only the inherited *possibility* of an idea and its symbol. It has no symbolic form until it assumes such form through the psychic process of projection. Such projection takes place as internal and environmental factors activate the archetype.

As noted earlier, much of Jung's analysis of the relationship between the archetype and its symbolic constellation is ambiguous. For example, what contribution the real mother makes in the Terrible Mother archetypal projection is unclear. On the one hand, the Terrible Mother is an archetype constellated in the infant's psyche and projected onto the real mother. In this case the infant does not necessarily experience its real mother as terrible. On the other hand, many causes of infantile neuroses can be traced to the mother. Jung concludes:

> The contents of the child's abnormal fantasies can be referred to the personal mother only in part, since they often contain clear and unmistakable allusions which could not possibly have reference to human beings. This is especially true when definitely mythological products are concerned, as is frequently the case in infantile phobias where the mother appears as a wild beast. . . . It must be born in mind, however, that such fantasies are not always of unmistakable mythological origin, and even if they are, they may not be rooted in the unconscious archetype. (1959, 83)

This suggests that only some parts of infantile fantasies may refer to the real mother. Other parts could refer to mythological products. The part of the fantasy that refers to the personal mother stems from a "more or less superficial layer of the unconscious, . . . the *personal unconscious*" (3). It is at this level of the unconscious that the particular "mother-complex" develops, for example, Don Juanism, homosexuality, or impotence, although "it is an open question whether a mother-complex can develop without the mother having taken part in its formation as a demonstrable causal factor" (85). Whether the actual mother is needed or not, the instinctual bipolar mother archetype, with its 'good' and 'terrible' aspects, can be constellated through the disturbance of the same archetype. It is these disturbances that "produce fantasies that come between the child and the mother as an alien and often frightening element" (85).

Although the question of the *role* of the mother in the formation of symbols representing the mother-complex remains open, Jung believes in the *fact* that the mother is needed for such formation. This belief is echoed by other Jungians. According to Erich

Neumann, whenever the generic (personal) mother deviates from the good Great Mother archetype, she also disturbs the archetypal constellation of the primal relationship between mother and infant. In some cases this can produce the archetypal negative primal relationship, which is "reflected by the rejection and condemnation of the Terrible Mother" (Neumann 1973, 42). If the mother is successful in constellating the Good Mother archetype, the child will be able to cope with stressful and fearful situations. Anthony Stevens (1982), drawing on a wealth of ethological evidence, supports the mythological examples explored by Jung and Neumann. The Terrible Mother will be constellated if the mother is resentful or hostile to the infant or if illness or accident renders her maternally inaccessible. Stevens, Neumann, and Jung fail to explore these disturbances from the point of view of culture's influence on the mother. Stevens concludes that "what matters from the point of view of healthy psychic development is not so much the actual behaviour and personality of the mother . . . *as the archetypal experiences actualized by her* in the child" (1982, 91).

Perhaps from the point of view of healthy psychic development, the actual mother (not the archetypal actualizer) is not necessary. Jung and Stevens exhibit in their respective work a certain ambivalence toward the mother. They appear unable to decide how the Terrible Mother comes to be constellated and symbolically expressed. Evidently there are parts of fantasies that may refer neither to the real mother nor to mythological origins nor to the unconscious archetype. What is this other reference point? A child has a fantasy of being devoured by a monster. It has a mythological quality to it. Perhaps it comes from a fairy tale, in which case it may not be rooted in the unconscious archetype of the child. Jung has not, in my opinion, made psychodynamic sense of the origins of symbols and their relation to culture (including fairy tales and rituals of sacrifice).

By way of conclusion, I want to comment on a significant similarity between Freud's patricidal and Jung's matricidal theory of sacrifice. While Freud's theory appears to require three objects (son, mother, father), the mother remains a passive object or prize of the struggle between father and son. In Jung's theory the actual mother's significance remains problematic, while the mother as a *symbol* of the unconscious is clearly more important. In spite of their efforts to differentiate from each other, on this matter of the mother (crucial in the very process of differentiation), Freud and Jung remain remarkably similar. Freud's and Jung's need to differentiate themselves from each other may have blinded them to the fundamental similarity between narcissism (Freud) and introversion (Jung), a point made by both Stein (1976, 46) and Homans (1979). As Homans points out, "when Jung spoke of a presexual stage given over to a sense of reality not composed entirely of sexual desire, he was referring to preoedipal narcissistic phenomena" (70). Indeed, in the 1912 edition of *Wadungen und Symbole der Libido*, Jung writes that the introversion of the mind was a "mother-child play with oneself . . . a Narcissus state" (70).

Both Freud and Jung were deeply concerned with the problem of narcissism at the time of their break. It is no coincidence that Jung's work on introversion in *Wadungen und Symbole der Libido* was attacked by Freud in his essay "On Narcissism" (1914) for Jung's indiscriminate application of the term *introversion*. Before 1914, the concept of narcissism was marginal to psychoanalytic theory. If, as Homans suggests, Freud and Jung were involved in narcissistic transferences with each other, this might explain why their theoretical work was focused at the time on such narcissistic issues. It might also explain why, as Kohut claims, "neither of the two grasped the enormous power of the narcissistic motivations in human relationships" (1978, 2:892).

EIGHT

Object Relations Theory: Illusion, Anxiety, and Symbols

I HAVE BEEN arguing that sacrifice is a ritual embodying male narcissistic anxiety about women. This theory consists of three elements to be correlated within a psychoanalytic point of view: symbol, anxiety, and women (and women as mothers). Both Freud's theory of sublimation and Jung's theory of creative introversion place the capacity of the mind to form symbols in the early years, even months, of life. Psychoanalysis has consistently, although at times ambivalently, held that there is an intimate correlation between the infant, the mother, and the symbol. Freud's early disciples (Adler, Jung, and Rank) broke with him, among other reasons, over the issue of the place of symbolization in the formation of the self within a psychoanalytic theory of personality and culture. Later work by Erich Fromm and Karen Horney (particularly in the area of dream imagery) emphasized the mind's capacity for symbolization as the key to understanding the development of the self. Freud, however, could not let go of the idea that dreams and fantasies were symbols of repressed infantile wishes. Any emphasis on symbolization as a central process in the development of the self remained unacceptable to him. In this chapter, I review two object relations theories of symbol formation that place the capacity to form symbols at the foundation of the psychological emergence and continuance of the self.

The development of the self is grounded in an increasingly complex capacity for symbolization. As Lifton expresses it, the self's development progresses from physiological inclination to enactment to inner imagery to symbolization (or psychoformation). . . .

Each takes shape initially in relation to bodily impulses and physical relationships to sources of nurturance and protection; each issues ultimately in complex adult capacities mediated by symbolization: capacities for participation in love and communal relationships, for moral and ethical commitment, and for maintaining a sense of self that includes symbolic development, growth, and change. (1976, 71)

In object relations theory and self-psychology, this capacity to form symbols develops as a result of several related psychological processes—idealization, internalization, and mourning. Idealization has its roots in the infant's treatment of external objects as though they were the ego. The infant idealizes these objects and internalizes them as aspects of the ego. As the child matures, the external objects lose some of their idealized quality, leading to some psychic disappointment. This idealized-object loss in turn leads to a process of mourning in which the idealized aspects of the lost object are transformed into the idealizations of the superego (Freud) and the self (object relations theory and self-psychology). This process of idealization is also the "main source of libidinal fuel for some of the socioculturally important activities which are subsumed under the term creativity" (Kohut 1971, 40). Taking this one step further, mourning is the chief process in the structural formation and transformation of symbols. This in turn leads to the conclusion by Homans that that mourning (de-idealization) is also "at the heart of the psychoanalytic view of religion" (1984, 135). If I understand with Geertz (1973) that religion is a cultural system, it is not only the theories of symbolization that are applicable to a social scientific theory of religion, but the psychological processes that characterize the formation of the self are applicable as well.

MELANIE KLEIN:
SYMBOLS OF PERSECUTION

THROUGH THE DEVELOPMENT of psychoanalytic play technique, a technique that sought access to the non-verbal world of the child, Melanie Klein began to suspect that there was evidence for earlier preoedipal fantasies and symbolic representations. In her interpretation of these fantasies and symbols, Klein believed that Freud's theory of the death instinct was correct and that the fear of death was the root of all persecutory anxiety. Freud had wondered why the superego was so much more severe than some actual parents. Klein suggested that reason lay in the relation between this severity and the death instinct. She theorized that during the first year of life the infant fantasizes both a good and a persecutory mother. She called this process of splitting the "paranoid-schizoid" period. Her hypothesis is that "the newborn baby experiences, both in the process of birth and in the adjustments to the post-natal situation, anxiety of a persecutory nature" (1963, 2). This feeling of anxiety is biological and exists from birth, if not earlier. The infant also has "an innate awareness of the mother" (2). These two experiences—persecution anxiety and awareness of the mother—become connected through the processes of projection and introjection: "Introjection means that the outer world, its impact, the situations the infant lives through, and the object he encounters, are not only experienced as external but are taken into the self and become part of his inner life. . . . Projection, which goes on simultaneously, implies that there is a capacity in the child to attribute to other people around him feelings of various kinds, predominantly love and hate" (5).

Together introjection and projection form the foundation for the infant's symbolic life. In the particular symbol of the mother I have been examining, the infant becomes frustrated and angry because he is hungry. Since he is innately aware of his mother, he projects that frustration and anger onto his mother (or her breast). The breast now has the qualities of frustration and anger. Through introjection the breast is re-experienced as an angry breast. The infant hallucinates that in his anger he is actually attacking and destroying the breast (the introjection). The infant simultaneously experiences his own anger and his screams as the breast attacking him (the projection).

Through the process of projection, the infant gains the impression that the breast, originally experienced as part of the infant, has been taken away from him. In this initial illusion the infant's desire for the breast and its appearance fosters a second illusion that the infant creates the breast when he needs it. If the breast does not appear soon enough, the frustration and anger occur and the breast is punished (the introjection) and then feared (the projection). In this sense the Terrible Mother occurs quite naturally as part of the development and eventual weaning of the infant. In fact, the process of introjection and projection, begun in the infant's relation to the mother, is the basis of all subsequent symbol formation. For Klein, the Terrible Mother fantasy and symbolic representations appear to be grounded in innate, epigenetic structures. Klein believes the fantasies are instinctual; indeed, fantasy is the "psychic representation of instinct" (6).

In Klein's view, a psychodynamic process of deprivation, rage, fear, envy, and gratitude in the infant is necessary for symbol formation. Underlying this sequence of psychological events, the identification of one object with another forms the basis of symbol formation. Following the lead of Ferenczi, she writes that "identification, the forerunner of symbolism, arises out of the baby's endeavor to rediscover in every object his own organs and their function" (1986, 97). But Klein builds on Ferenczi's position by arguing that anxiety (persecutory anxiety) begins the process of identification. "This anxiety contributes to make him equate the organs in question with other things; owing to this equation these in their turn become objects of anxiety, and so he is impelled constantly to make other and new equations, which form the basis of his interest in the new objects and of symbolism" (97).

Klein supports Freud's position that this symbolism is the basis of all sublimation. Yet how does persecutory anxiety lead to the identification of one object with another? Is the fusion of one object with another simply the basis for renewed anxiety? In other words, is symbolism always defensive? And, perhaps more importantly, how is anxiety transformed into symbol? What seems to be missing from Klein's theory is a means of creating the symbol. What it needs is "a medium between the self-created [illusion] and external realities [objects]" (Milner 1955, 98). Marion Milner's point is well taken. Her conclusion is that the medium (illusion, play, etc.) is in fact the basis for the psychological structure leading to symbols, a point explored by Winnicott.

FREUD, JUNG, AND KLEIN: BIOLOGISTS IN NEED OF A "GOOD-ENOUGH" MOTHER

KLEIN, LIKE FREUD and Jung, tried to account for symbol formation and the symbol of the Terrible Mother through a theory of instinctual representations. All three grounded the Terrible Mother in biologically innate instincts and experiences. Jung considered the archetype to be an inherited biological potentiality, ambiguously dependent on the experience of the mother for its actualization. He attempted to distinguish symbolic representations of the instinctual archetype from abnormal fantasies resembling the archetype, thereby accounting for the differences by appealing to two levels of the unconscious: the personal and the collective. Freud believed the fantasy of the devouring mother to be based on the ambivalent experience of narcissistic differences and oedipal differentiation. The male infant fears that the mother envies his penis and could castrate him for it. Later the fear is transferred to the father in the incest-castration complex. The fantasy (idea) is a repression of two instinctual drives: the urge to return to the womb (represented by the death instinct and the experience of the uncanny) and the urge to penetrate the womb (incest). The actual genders of the mother and the infant play a significant biological function in the development of fantasy and symbol.

Klein stands midway between Freud and Jung. She recognizes the instinctual nature of fantasy. But the fantasy is not sexual (in the sense of gender or genitalia), nor is it only an instinctual potentiality. The introjection and projection of the devouring breast is essential in the creation of the self and self-awareness. Such a fantasy stems from frustration and leads, through introjection, to envy, fear, and guilt: the superego. Such a theory sees fantasy and symbol formation as representative of instincts. Unlike Jung, there is no effort to distinguish between abnormal and instinctual fantasies. Certain traumas can, however, calcify the split between good and bad mother to the point of pathology.

Because all three remain biologists of the mind, however, their theories of the relation between mother and infant and symbol formation fall somewhat short. Klein missed because she projected onto infants a psychological structure more likely found in children and adults. Do infants themselves experience persecution? Jung's theory remains irritatingly vague. It switches from archetype to symbol to instinct too indiscriminately. And, more to the point, it offers no clear explanation of the relation between the developing psyche and culture. Culture is more than a screen on which are projected symbolic representations of archetypes of the collective unconscious. Freud's useful discussion of sublimation and identification is lost when it attempts to understand the symbol of the terrible woman or her cultural degradation. In short, I believe all three fail to take more seriously the affective relationship between a mother and her infant and the analytic reactivation of the psychodynamic structures developed as a result of such affect. Nevertheless, clearly all three know that the developing psyche's ability to form symbols is centered on the relation between infant and mother. I am, therefore, a bit closer to understanding a relation between infant and mother, but still quite some distance from a psychoanalytic relation between women and sacrifice. Between the male experience of women and the male ritual of sacrifice lies a third order of experience, one that Freud, Jung, and Klein have recognized but only partially developed.

D. W. WINNICOTT:
TRANSITIONAL OBJECTS, ILLUSION, AND SYMBOL FORMATION

WINNICOTT WROTE EXTENSIVELY on the developmental importance of the mother-infant relation, and he has provided a theory of the psychological structure that makes possible the formation of the symbol and the self. Winnicott was not the first to emphasize the clinical importance of the difference between the reality of the mother and the infant's (or analysand's) image of her. Freud recognized the obvious and significant difference between them, noting, for example, that the superego often appears more severe than the mother's or father's moral expectations (1923, 52–53). If the superego is capable of doing this, then some inner psychic image must be available to the superego, for how else could it display such severity? Of course Freud could have been mistaken. He based his insights on the analysis of adults. How could such analyses reveal every possible image with which to judge severity? Whatever the plausibility of such an insight, Winnicott's observation of infants during his career as both pediatrician and analyst tend to confirm Freud's remarks.

But Winnicott was more interested in developing a theory of the context within which fantasy operates. To begin with the obvious, the term *fantasy* implies a correlative reality. In his theory of the developing individual's view and conception of the external factors, Winnicott assumed that a "good-enough mother" provides the basis for all subsequent ability to conceptualize reality. The good-enough mother adapts actively to the needs of the infant. As the infant grows, the infant's developing psychological apparatus is increasingly able to accept and handle the frustrations of incomplete adaptation on the part of the mother. Being good-enough means that "this adaptation demands an easy and unresented preoccupation with the one infant; in fact, success in the infant's care depends on the fact of devotion, not on cleverness or intellectual enlightenment" (1971a, 10).

The mother's task, then, is to gradually disillusion the infant. She has no hope of success unless first she has been able to give sufficient opportunity for illusion. The degree of adaptation by the mother is highly significant and central to Winnicott's concept of the good-enough mother. Such adaptation needs to be nearly exact at the beginning of the infant's life. The extent to which this occurs determines how well the infant develops a capacity for experiencing a relation to external reality or even for forming a symbolic representation of that reality. A good-enough mother, by adapting at or near 100 percent to the immediate needs of the infant, allows the infant the illusion that there are no needs. The initial illusion that there are no needs is maintained through the fact that with near-100 percent adaptation the time/space difference between need (i.e., for the breast) and satisfaction are nearly one in the same thing, at least from the illusory point of view of the infant. Without adequate adaptation, there can be no illusion. The primary illusion is that the infant and mother are one. The illusion that the mother's breast is the infant corresponds to the illusion of omnipotence. Ferenczi points out that "omnipotence [is the] feeling that one has all that one wants and that one has nothing left to wish for" (1956, 183). The infant's illusion is not simply that he has all he needs; he does not even need to need. Indeed the *he* that needs is not part of his experience: "*nothing has yet been separated out as not-me*, so there is *not yet a* **ME**" (Winnicott 1965a, 17).

In this period of primary narcissism (Winnicott avoids many references to narcissism), omnipotence is experienced as reality, or, "omnipotence is nearly a fact of experience" (1971a, 11). Of course this omnipotent illusion and its initial developmental stage do not last. Eventually the good-enough mother disillusions the infant. This may not be something she is consciously trying to do. But as the need for the breast occurs, the degree of adaptation gradually lessens and the narcissistic illusion that the infant and the breast are the same is replaced with the infant's illusion that he has created the breast:

At some theoretical point early in the development of every human individual an infant in a certain setting provided by the mother is capable of conceiving of the idea of something that would meet the growing need that arises out of instinctual tension. The infant cannot be said to know at first what is to be created. At this point in time the mother presents herself. In the ordinary way she gives her breast and her potential feeling urges. The mother's adaptation to the infant's needs, when good-enough, gives the infant the *illusion* that there is an external reality that corresponds to the infant's own capacity to create. (11–12)

Winnicott has not said that the infant merely perceives the breast is there. Such a perception is secondary. Initially the illusion mediates between the reality of the breast and instinctual tensions (e.g., hunger). The infant draws in the milk that he has created. The mother provides the setting for the creation of a mediating illusion of reality, which is different from later perceptions of that reality. This concept of the initial mediating illusion is the basis of Winnicott's theory of transitional objects and transitional phenomena. The good-enough mother provides the initial "facilitating environment," which makes possible the development of later mature capacities to recognize, accept, and relate to reality (1965b, 223).

In a closer look at the image of the mother, Winnicott's theory of illusion and fantasy is somewhat different from Freud's theory of the infantile ideation of "mother" based on projection. As projection it remains a creation of the infant. Winnicott's transitional object theory introduces the idea of the actual facilitating environment regardless of projection. Creating an image, then, is not so much a projection as it is a transitional phenomenon. That is, the image is neither a projection (Freud) nor an internal object (Klein), rather it is a possession. In order to create an image (a fantasy, later a symbol) of the mother, the infant's near-100 percent adaptive relationship with the object (e.g., breast) is destroyed. The breast becomes an object when the infant fantasizes its destruction.

First there is object-relating [infant and breast are not separate phenomena], then in the end there is object-use [infant feeds from an other-than-me]; in between, however, is the most difficult thing, perhaps, in human development; or the most irksome of all the early failures that come from mending [i.e., psychoanalysis or other therapy]. This thing that there is between

relating and use is the subject's placing of the object outside the
area of the subject's omnipotent control; that is, the subject's
perception of the object as an external phenomenon, not as a
projective entity, in fact recognition of it as an entity in its own
right. (89–90)

While the process of projection may help in determining what
is there, the projection is not the initial reason for that object now
always being experienced as distinct. Rather, the fantasy of destroying the object (when successful) places the object outside of the subject. Winnicott acknowledged that access to these fantasies evolved
through the observation of infant and child play. From such observations he, as Klein before him, concluded that the ability to place
the object outside of the subject involves paradoxically a fantasized
destruction of the object. This is what Klein termed the archaic fantasies to devour the breast and the resulting fear from reprisals. According to Winnicott, the infant passes from object-relating to object-use with the fantasy that the object is destroyed by the subject:
"the destruction plays the part in making the reality, placing the object outside the self" (17). The infant psychologically survives the
creation of object and subject through transitional objects and transitional phenomena. Among the objects are such things as pieces of
fuzzy cloth or a diaper used in conjunction with sucking the thumb,
for example. The pattern is personal to the child, and this pattern,
which appears at the time of going to sleep or at times of loneliness,
sadness, or anxiety, may persist into late childhood or even adult life.
Transitional objects and phenomena "exist" in the psychological space
that once held the illusion of non-differentiation between the infant
as subject and the mother as object, as well as the illusion that the
mother (breast) was created by the infant.

This "potential space" is the foundation for play and then the
cultural experience of the individual. The potential space of play, of
creativity, of the creation of or psychological resonance with cultural
symbols depends on the infant's experience of the transition from
pure subjectivity to the me/not-me split (from illusion to omnipotence—magical thinking, to transitional objects and phenomena, to
play, to cultural experience). The optimal experience is one of trust
or confidence in the midst of potential anxiety.

> The potential space between baby and mother, between child
> and family, between individual and society or the world, de-

pends on experience that leads to trust. It can be looked upon
as sacred to the individual in that it is here that the individual
experiences creative living.

By contrast, exploitation of this area leads to a pathological
condition in which the individual is cluttered up with persecutory elements of which he has no means of ridding himself. (103)

Since the cause of certain psychopathologies relates to disturbances
in the "potential space," one function of psychoanalysis (and psy-
chotherapy in general) is to provide a facilitating environment in which
the "journey of progress towards experience" (i.e., through transitional objects such as analysts) can take place. Likewise, the "Squiggle
Game," in which a drawing developed mutually by therapist and child
client provides a medium for psychodynamic expression. "It is almost
as if the child, through the drawings, is along side me, and to some
extent taking part in describing the case, so that the reports of what
the child and the therapist said tend to ring true" (1971b, 3). Without denying the necessity of making such a normative assessment of
mirroring trust or human exploitation, Winnicott's theory of the origins
of cultural experience goes far in helping us understand the relations
between the infant and the mother and culture, including religion
and religious symbols such as sacrifice. Exploitation of that relationship has occurred and continues to occur. If, as I and others have
argued, there are actual and/or symbolic expressions of anxiety contained in sacrifice, then the need to explain the origins of that anxiety
remains the burden of this book. Whether that anxiety is persecutory,
whether it stems from the potential space of a mother and her infant
remains to be seen. If Winnicott is correct, however, the potential
space remains a "place" where subsequent illusions of omnipotence,
fantasies, and fears could be played out with bloody consequences.
How can I answer that question? As in the other theories of symbol
formation, I argue that the answer involves a look at how Winnicott
analyzes and explains the cultural fear and degradation of women.

Winnicott reported that "in the unconscious fantasy of people
in general, the most awful ideas cluster round the infant-mother relationship" (1986, 248). Is this a tendency unique to the psychological West? Or, as Winnicott suspects, is there some evidence that such
fantasies are more widespread, indeed "universal"? (252). The fear
of women stems from the no-longer-remembered debt to a particular
woman—a mother, although the dread is of WOMAN; "the fear of

WOMAN represents the first stage of this acknowledgement" (252). In a footnote on the same page Winnicott notes the following: "It would be out of place to discuss this here in detail, but the idea can be reached best if approached gradually: (i) Fear of the parents of very early childhood. (ii) Fear of a combined figure, a woman with male potency in her powers (witch). (iii) Fear of the mother who has absolute power at the beginning of the infant's existence to provide, or fail to provide, the essentials for the early establishment of the self as an individual" (252 n. 1). If traced to its roots, "this fear of WOMAN turns out to be a fear of recognizing the fact of dependence" (252). The psychological reason men and women fear WOMAN is the basis of the psychology of tyranny:

> *One of the roots of the need to be a dictator can be a compulsion to deal with this fear of woman by encompassing her and acting for her.* The dictator's curious habit of demanding not only absolute obedience and absolute dependence but also "love" can be derived from this source.
>
> Moreover, the tendency of groups of people to accept or even seek *actual* domination is derived from a fear of domination by *fantasy woman*. This fear leads them to seek, and even welcome, domination by a known human being, especially one who has taken on himself the burden of personifying and therefore limiting the magical qualities of the all-powerful woman of fantasy, to whom is owed the great debt. The dictator can be overthrown, and eventually must die; but the woman figure of primitive unconscious fantasy has no limits to her existence or power. (253)

Winnicott is making a crucial point: the object of the fear is not a particular woman, yet it clearly grows out of particular relationships with particular women (mothers). Winnicott is saying that the fear is of an image, a fantasy, an idea, perhaps even a transitional object. The object of the fear is not the illusion of an object created by the subject. But it has something to do with it. Men fear something they have created yet somehow that image reflects something experienced as well. The question still remains, How does the fear or anxiety arise? Does the fear of Woman have its origin in the preoedipal period of transitional objects? Winnicott certainly thinks so. But does this theory of anxiety sufficiently explain why male anxiety about women is expressed in sacrifice and why only men have sacrificed? I think that Winnicott's failure to take into account the gender of mothers and sons in his delineation of transitional anxiety leads to a significant and faulty conclusion. By this failure to see the importance of gender, Winnicott unwittingly rationalizes the oppression of women carried out by men as in some way expressing a fear of women held by both men *and* women. Men are therefore punishing the mothers on behalf of the daughters as well as on behalf of themselves as sons. But is this the case? Men do not sacrifice in order to give the power from women (mothers) to other women. They sacrifice to exclude women from this power. As I argue in Part III, the role of gender in the development of gender-specific anxiety is crucial to understanding sacrifice. Winnicott has taken a step closer than Klein in understanding that anxiety, but in the end he leaves little clinical evidence for such gender-specific anxiety.

NINE

Two Contemporary Psychoanalytic Theories of Sacrifice

THE DISCUSSIONS ABOUT the psychological dimensions of ritual and symbol in the preceding three chapters have been based on the theoretical insights of clinicians, from Freud to Winnicott. While Freud and others have been interested in the psychology of sacrifice, the development of a psychoanalytic component has not been limited to clinicians. But the subject matter of ritual sacrifice is not strictly derived at the analytic couch, although its psychology may be powerfully suggested there or in other clinical settings. Sacrifice has a subtle texture, which is part of the historical fabric of cultures, and the psychology of sacrifice must be contextualized within that fabric. Thus, while psychoanalysts may venture into the history of religions to explore sacrifice, like Freud they may have to struggle with the methodological context for their exploration. The opposite is true as well. Historians of culture have been drawn to the insights of psychoanalysis as a welcome addition for more fully contextualized insights about sacrifice. In this chapter I present and critique two recent theories of sacrifice that make use of psychoanalytic thought, those of René Girard and Eli Sagan.

RENÉ GIRARD: SACRIFICE AND MIMETIC DESIRE

GIRARD (1977) ATTEMPTS AN interpretation of sacrifice that bridges the gap between anthropological and psychoanalytic theories of sacrifice. Girard agrees with Turner (1969) that in ritual, communitas has the liminal effect of minimizing distinctions between classes of people or of making such distinctions more ambiguous. In the elimination of distinctions, however, imitative or mimetic quality to ritual actions becomes apparent. Men will act like women, women like men, slaves like masters, people like animals, humans like gods, etc. An example of men imitating women is graphically displayed in certain Aztec sacrifices in which the priests wear the flayed skins of sacrificed women. This mimetism is not restricted to the symbolic replication of action, but includes the orectic desires that motivate those actions. Imitation is done so out of desire for what is imitated—desire for desired objects ("objects" in a psychological sense). Among an undifferentiated group desiring the same object, tensions and conflicts may erupt in the form of envy and rivalry. Such rivalry, according to Girard's theory, may lead to violent consequences.

Girard further suggests that the violent aspect of sacrifice not only reflects the potential violence of undifferentiation (liminality), but also provides the opportunity for that violence to be acted out in a culturally sanctioned form. Thus, Girard attempts to move beyond the description of the symbolic structure to an explanation of sacrifice that places the violence of the act at the heart of the ritual. According to his theory, the reason people experience the transversal of margins or the elimination of distinctions as a threat is not simply because they violate symbolic classifications (Mary Douglas's theory). More fundamentally, the elimination of distinction leads to rivalry, which in turn leads to violence due to the tendency to maim or kill a rival in order to possess a mutually desired object. "Order, peace, and fecundity," writes Girard, "depend on cultural distinctions; it is not these distinctions but the loss of them that gives rise to fierce rivalries and sets members of the same family or social group at one another's throats" (1977, 49). The function of sacrifice is to channel the equivocal danger of and desire for violence onto a surrogate victim. The destruction takes away the violent danger while at the same time giving expression to the violence. The use of the surrogate victim avoids any reciprocity for the violence because the victim represents a socially marginal and liminal being, that is, the victim possesses no effective retaliatory power.

As noted in Chapter 6, Girard argues that the Oedipus complex contains elements of mimetic desire, which Freud suppressed. Because the child imitates his idealized father, Girard reasons, the son desires the mother because the father desires her. The father, not the child, perceives the rivalry and reacts with threats of violence. Freud, on the other hand, argued that because "the little boy's father is perceived as an obstacle, his identification takes on a hostile colouring and changes into a wish to get rid of the father" (1923, 32–33). Girard presents these as opposing positions and is unhappy with Freud's "refuge in the idea of ambivalence" to explain the origins of the oedipal conflict (1977, 182). That is, Freud finally argued for the origins of desire and dread within the child alone. Bakan also claims that "the Oedipus complex might itself be a reaction of the child to the infanticidal impulse of the father" (1968, 104). This position has merit for understanding the psychology of sacrifice. But Girard seems more interested in disproving Freud than in answering his own questions about violence and the sacred. Because Freud's metapsychology is incomplete, Girard believes he can replace the Oedipus complex with mimetic desire and eliminate repression and the unconscious as well (1977, 183). By eliminating Freud, however, Girard has not explained why a child seeks to imitate his father in the first place. The origins of mimetic desire do not lie in an infant's idealization of his father, any more than a male infanticidal impulse lies in a father's rivalry with his son. Both have their psychological origins in a more archaic, preoedipal experience of an infant and his mother. Both the infant and the adult male envy (desire) and fear the woman as mother. When understood in the light of preoedipal psychology, the object of mimetic desire is the mother, not because the father desires her, but because of the infant's and adult's narcissistic relation to her.

Girard was aware that Freud's metapsychology was incomplete. Yet it was not so incomplete that Freud did not try to understand the relation among identification, idealization, and narcissism, as noted in chapter 6. But Girard offers no mythological or psychoanalytic references connecting mimetic desire and narcissistic identification. There is, nevertheless, a strong affinity between Girard's idea of mimetic desire and Freud's idea of secondary narcissistic identification. Surprisingly, Girard avoids any mention of Freud's essay "On Narcissism," which is among the first efforts to address the subjects of idealization, identification, and introjection. While his impatience with Freud is understandable, Girard's failure to see the question of idealization, identification, and anxiety within a narcissistic context clouds the issue as much for him as for Freud. That failure leaves unsatisfactory his theory of sacrifice.

ELI SAGAN: SACRIFICE AND PREOEDIPAL DEVELOPMENT

WITH INTERESTS VERY similar to Girard, Sagan has written several books (1974, 1979, 1985) on the theory and origin of male violence and oppression. Unlike Girard, Sagan recognizes preoedipal identification and anxiety in the psychological structure of human sacrifice. He notes three processes in particular. The first is taken from Anna Freud's idea of "identification with the aggressor" (A. Freud 1973, 109–16). When confronted by an external aggressor, the ego identifies with the aggressor and changes from the one about to be destroyed to the destroyer. Sagan adds to this what he calls "identification with the aggressor by making someone else the victim" (1985, 351). The fear of an aggressor (imagined or real) is, in Sagan's view, the reason why those who control societies seek victims to sacrifice. "If all human societies, up until today, have persevered in the necessity of having victims, it can only be that those who control societies are so deeply frightened that they can only feel better by seeing that others are brought down" (351–52). Sagan claims that Auschwitz and the cutting of welfare payments in American society are of the same *dis*order. "Someone must suffer or die so that I can breathe again" (352).

The second psychological process that helps explain the psychology of human sacrifice is that of "beating on someone in order to combat the repressed within oneself" (352). Sagan notes that in present-day America, the brutalization of homosexuals is of this psychological order. "It is the fear of impotence among the 'strong' that causes society to trample on those who are defenseless" (352).

Because Sagan is concerned with why human sacrifice occurs only in those societies that had changed from a kinship system to a kingship system, he theorizes that the highest members of a society went through a psychological process of extricating themselves from the kinship system. Both individually and collectively these aristocrats experienced a severe separation anxiety. Ambivalent about whether to actually separate from the "cozy ambience of kinship solidarity" (352), the individuating aristocrat would have felt both the urge to continue and the urge to return. Aware of the power and prestige that is the prize for forward movement, the aristocrat repressed the regressive urge by destroying its representation or projection in others, those who had not yet begun the process of kinship extrication.

To accomplish this meant killing a representative of the kinship system—"a man who has not even begun to liberate himself from kinship attachments, a man who stands for all the cowardly, childish, womanish longings within oneself—and to cut his throat as an offering for the gods" (352).

The third mechanism of human sacrifice is "the concept that, in certain situations of stress, one thing can substitute for another" (353). Played out in human sacrifice through the substitution of one person for another, the process of substitution is not limited to human sacrifice but occurs in all forms of sacrifice and other rituals. Symbolic substitution works because of the related processes of identification and illusion, although as anthropologists have often pointed out, the participants are rarely under the illusion that the substitution is as literal as the symbol suggests.

With these psychological processes and the historical fact that societies did change from kinship system to complex kingship systems (where one kinship group exercised political power over larger, non-kinship groups), Sagan pondered "the mystery of why, the road being so difficult, any society would set out on the journey away from the kinship system in the first place" (353). To answer that question Sagan turns to the psychoanalytic work of Margaret Mahler (1968; Mahler, Pine, and Bergman 1975), because in the social process from kinship to individualism, he sees a parallel psychic process of separation and individuation.

Mahler, with Winnicott and Kohut, represent a psychoanalytic theory that places much, if not more, importance on the preoedipal period of infant development. The separation-individuation process, which she has developed from her observation of infants and children, has three stages: autism, symbiosis, and separation-individuation. Autism (birth to one month) is characterized by a complete lack of differentiation. There is, from the infant's psychological experience, no difference between it and its mother, between its mouth and the breast. During this period the infant gradually experiences varying degrees of differentiation, so that by the symbiotic stage (one to six months) it becomes aware that it and the mother are different, yet existence apart from the mother is psychologically inconceivable.

During the separation-individuation stage (six to thirty months) the child not only recognizes that it is different from the mother, but separates from her and thus individuates itself. Sagan contends that the response of the parents and society to the child during this stage are of paramount importance. Any number of a variety of responses is possible. Responses may be encouraging, discouraging, encouraging then discouraging, depending on the type of society, its stage of development, and the type of socialization practiced. For example, "in a society where all children are nursed for four years, a child will spend the whole of the separation-individuation stage nursing and will have a profoundly different experience from a child in a society prescribing that he be weaned at six to twelve months" (Sagan 1985, 355).

Mahler divided the separation-individuation stage into four subphases: differentiation (six to ten months); practicing (ten to eighteen months); rapprochement (eighteen to twenty-four months); and consolidation of individuality (twenty-four to thirty months). In the differentiation subphase, the child begins to experience itself as separate from the mother. The growing awareness of separateness is followed by the practicing subphase, during which "libidinal cathexis shifts substantially into the service of the rapidly growing autonomous ego and its functions, and the child seems intoxicated with his own faculties and with the greatness of his world. Narcissism is at its peak!" (Mahler, Pine, and Bergman 1985, 71). After the practicing subphase comes the rapprochement crisis, marked by an increase in separation anxiety. "As the toddler's *awareness* of separation grows . . . he seems to have an increased need, a wish for mother to share with him every one of his new skills and experiences, as well as a great need for the object's love" (76–77).

The rapprochement crisis is the critical period of the separation-individuation process because that is when progress toward individuality and/or regression back towards less self differentiation is very possible, depending on the kind and quality of parental care. The period is marked by great ambivalence on the part of the toddler (if not the parent). The toddler enjoys his grandiosity yet fears separation, and at the same time, the toddler enjoys the parental connection yet fears re-engulfment by the mother. Notice here that Mahler recognized both forms of anxiety with which Freud and Jung struggled, and that she located both fears within the same developmental phase. In this phase the child's relationship with the father becomes more focused and important in the resolution of the rapprochement crisis. The consistent image of a father or other non-maternal figure is necessary as a counterbalance to the toddler's re-engulfment anxiety. Mahler argues for a more positive image and role for the father in the development of the child. He is not to be thought of simply as the castrating character, but as a positive developmental force in the process of individuation. Without his and the mother's support in this period, Mahler argues, "a re-engulfment of the ego into the whirlpool of the primary undifferentiated symbiotic stage becomes a true threat" (145).

Sagan's theory of human sacrifice is predicated on the assumption that human societies have evolved in a fashion that parallels and is affected by individual, psychological development. For the most part this assumption awaits further exploration for the simple reason that the vast majority of ethnographies available have such a paucity of information regarding child-rearing practices. In the meantime, however, Sagan suggests the following scenario:

> During the rapprochement crisis, primitive society closes in on the whole separation-individuation process; it emphasizes separation anxiety, indulges in quasi-symbiotic relationships with the mother by means of a long breast-feeding period and the extended sleeping arrangements of mother and child, represses individuation and individuality, and maintains the kinship system as the social form that certifies a nonindividuated political life. The refusal to proceed fully with the separation-individuation process leads to an underdeveloped Oedipal phase, thus maintaining the pre-Oedipal nature of primitive society: its lack of fully developed anthropomorphic gods; its use of shame and the absence of guilt; its vague relationship to conscience; its failure to develop advanced political forms. (1985, 362)

Some of these elements are recognizable in the descriptions by Douglas and especially Geertz (although the child-rearing accounts are, as noted, absent). The importance of *buhonyi* (which Douglas translates as a combination of shame, shyness, and modesty) and *hama* (dread) among the Lele and that of *lek* (which Geertz calls "stage fright" bordering on aesthetic dread among the Balinese) are both suggestive of the preoedipal affect about which Sagan has written. In many Melanesian societies, particularly those in the eastern Papua New Guinea highlands, the image Sagan paints seems applicable. These societies with kinship systems as their main organizing principle are more than likely to have animal blood sacrifice (if they have sacrifice), as opposed to human sacrifices.

Complex society, on the other hand, is much more in the middle of the rapprochement crisis. In complex society some individuals have managed to individuate out of the kinship symbiosis, but there is, as noted above, a fear of the power of the system out of which they have individuated—the fear of re-engulfment. Children are often raised away from the home—one thinks of the gymnasiums of ancient Greece—in order to avoid the regressive urge to re-engulfment. Human sacrifice becomes the ultimate symbolic expression of the fear of re-engulfment. The king, possessing absolute tyrannical power, embodies the "temper-tantrum behavior" of the ambivalent rapprochement phase. In this stage the child projects its own desire for re-engulfment onto the mother, so that she is the one who wants to merge again; she becomes the one who brings about the regression. Therefore, she and her representation in the kinship system have to be destroyed in order to overcome her seductive power. Sagan concludes that "there was once a stage of human society, not psychotic, but threatened by re-engulfment by the kinship system, and it ritually slaughtered its own people by the thousands" (363).

Sagan is offering a powerful psychoanalytic theory of history and culture worth considering. In his theory of sacrifice, he has seen the intimate connection between kinship system and sacrifice, and he has suggested how both sacrifice and kinship systems are to a great extent preoedipal. The adult dread of re-engulfment into the kinship system is a cultural transformation of the toddler's dread of re-engulfment into the mother. The victims of human sacrifice are marginal, powerless people who represent both the maternal and kinship matrix out of which the individuated aristocrat has extricated himself. When men sacrifice, they are saying NO to the mother. Sagan's theory ends up very close to Jung's (as does Mahler's).

But this theory has some difficulties. First, with regard to kinship and kinship systems, Sagan makes no attempt to understand the difference between matrilineal and patrilineal descent. He treats them equally when he claims that kinship (matriliny or patriliny) represents the mother (or vice versa). Some primitive societies are matrilineal (such as the Lele studied by Douglas) and perform no sacrifices. Some are patrilineal (the Nuer and Dinka) and perform sacrifices. Some are mixed—matrilineal and patrilineal—and perform sacrifices (the Malekulans) or rituals that may or may not be considered sacrifices (the circumcision rituals of the Ndembu studied by Turner). What seems clear, as Jay (1985) convincingly argues, is that when it serves patrilineal functions, sacrifice elevates patriliny over against matriliny. Psychologically, what does sacrifice have to do with the relation between patriliny and matriliny? On this Sagan is silent. Second, he does not distinguish between animal sacrifices in primitive (kinship system) societies and later complex and archaic societies. At one point he states that animal sacrifice replaced human sacrifice in advanced complex societies (1985). But he does not explain how it is that the Nuer and Dinka (both primitive kinship societies) practice animal sacrifice. Did they practice human sacrifice previously? And, if human sacrifice is a consequence of extrication from kinship systems and passage to complex kingship systems, does this mean that Nuer and Dinka societies are regressive because they practice animal sacrifice? The ethnographic evidence does not support such a conclusion. Sacrifice in patrilineal kinship systems is not a cultural regression. There is a connection between animal and human sacrifice and it does have to do with descent, but its logic is not to be discovered strictly in the transition from kinship to kingship.

Third, by using Mahler, Sagan cannot truly account for the formation of cultural symbols out of the separation-individuation process. "Our lack of theoretical structure," laments Sagan, "makes it impossible to say how the symbolic forms . . . relate to the modes of attachment" (221). Likewise, Mahler's work with children and infants leaves her interpretation open to the complaint of adultomorphism, that is, her observations of pre-oedipal behavior remain interpreted from an adult point of view. She has no way of systematically confirming her observations, by either slipping into the mind of the infant or asking the infant to confirm her interpretation (her interpretive observation). Thus, "fear of re-engulfment" is an adult projection onto the infant's psychological apparatus. How well does the adult fear of re-engulfment correspond to the infant's own inner life? And is such fear the most accurate meaning of the adult man's inner, and still active, preoedipal life?

Sagan's work is, nevertheless, thoughtful and originative, and it contributes to the psychology of sacrifice in a way that Girard's cannot because it makes the necessary connection between preoedipal narcissism and sacrifice. But its reliance on the "fear of re-engulfment" as the narcissistic fuel for male rage against the maternal is only a half truth—it is, in my opinion, too narrow, too mythical, and too grandiose (my criticism of Jung's theory was similar), and it relies on adultomorphic projections. To achieve a more accurate portrayal of the infantile past requires the mind of an adult who is allied with his analyst in the discovery of those infant psychological structures reactivated in the transferences. A theory of narcissism that comes out of *that* work would seem more likely to understand the narcissistic rage of sacrifice. Kohut's psychology of narcissism is such a theory.

TEN

Psychoanalysis in Search of a Theory of Culture

IN CONSTRUCTING THE thesis of Part II that there is an intimate relationship between the male need for power and control, symbols that express that need (such as ritual sacrifice), and the mother-infant relation, I have explored psychological theories of how symbols are formed and acquired and how that process relates to particular cultural images (attitudes, fantasies, and symbols) of the mother. Each theory postulates various forms of anxiety: the dread (desire and fear) of incest (Freud), the fear of re-engulfment (Jung, Mahler), the persecutory fear of retaliation (Klein), and the fear of dependence (Winnicott). It might be argued that these are all variations on the theme of the fear of death, and I am attempting to understand the sense in which sacrifice expresses, embodies, and conceals such fear. Yet if sacrifice contains such functions, why is it that only men traditionally control the ritual sacrificial life of a community? Do only men fear death? As noted earlier, issues of gender specificity have often been ignored or minimized.

Only Freud's phenomenologically incomplete oedipal theory tries to explain why sacrifice is a male ritual, performed by men. Jungian and object relations theories assume that the preoedipal period is a pregender period. If sacrifice embodies such preoedipal psychological structures, what nonoedipal explanation might account for the gender dimension of sacrifice? The answer, as I suggested, begins with Freud's explanation of men's disdain for women, "the narcissistic rejection of women by men, which is so much mixed up with despising them" (Freud 1918, 199). Freud's *two* reasons why men fear women reveal his keen self-analytic eye. Men fear being castrated (first by the mother, then by the father), which, as we have seen, is only an intermediate explanation. But they also fear because women are *different*. In other words, men fear women for narcissistic reasons, not strictly for oedipal or phallic reasons. But, as we have also seen, Freud's theory of sublimation (and narcissism) cannot adequately account for the symbolization of such fear. Nevertheless, if the fear is preoedipal, there has to be a means of applying a gender dimension, which may be eroticized (telescoped) onto later developmental stages.

But there is a more profound problem with these theories. They remain psychodynamic theories without an adequate theory of culture. Freud (unlike Klein) provides a theoretical structure for realizing the relation between the identification with and internalization of cultural objects. And his incomplete theory of narcissism (via identification, idealization, sublimation, melancholia, and even the uncanny) opens the way to understanding the psychological structure embodied in such cultural objects. In theory the emphasis is not on the instinctual drives (the id), but on the ego, which "owes its origins as well as most of its acquired characteristics to its relation to the real external world" (Freud 1940, 201). Yet his emphasis remains on the individual psychic apparatus and not on the forces of cultural objects. This is why his metapsychology fails.

Winnicott's object relational theory provides evidence for the medium through which such an apparatus identifies with and internalizes the meaning of cultural objects (via the good-enough environment, trust, transitional objects and transitional phenomena, play, and culture). Yet the reliance on too narrow a structure of anxiety leaves many activities of sacrifice unexplained. The main consequence of the shift in developmental theories from drive or impulse to object relations, however, is that the sociocultural world becomes increasingly significant.

Fred Weinstein and Gerald Platt emphasize that "in the larger sense personality is built up and organized on the basis of identification with, and internalization of, patterns of behavior transmitted by emotionally significant persons" (1973, 16). I have been arguing that identification and internalization by means of a transitional psychological process originates in the infant's evolving relation with the mother. But, as Erik Erikson claims, personality is more than the sum total of the identifications of childhood (1968, 158). Nevertheless, while identification is only partially useful in the psychoanalytic and sociological sense, it remains the basic apparatus for an ego psychology of personality. Would it be safe to say that identification and idealization form the psychological foundation of Durkheim's central idea of "sentimental affinity," the basis of classification and social structure? Through identification and internalization, the personality is able to grow in both self-identity and self-worth (provided the idealized cultural objects identified with and internalized are sufficiently self-enhancing). And identity and self-esteem are, according to Weinstein and Platt, "ultimately tied to social membership (i.e., to status within groups and institutions) and hence to the external world" (1973, 82). Furthermore, the development of identity that "accompanies the oedipal resolution implies a movement from a world of objects to a world of symbols" (82). In Winnicott's terms, this development implies a shift from object relating to object use. Using Erikson's understanding of identity, Weinstein and Platt state that individual identity "refers to the organization of patterns of behavior . . . which enable the individual to deal with, and adapt to ongoing and conflicting internal and external situations" (87).

In addition to identification and internalization, Weinstein and Platt state that object loss is the other aspect of an object relations theory of individual and group identity embodied in "obligated patterns of expression" (87). These obligated patterns of expression would presumably include both religious codes and ritual activities, including sacrifice. By "object loss," they mean "the normatively perceived passing or failure of, disappointment in, abandonment or betrayal by loved or otherwise valued persons, institutions, symbols, and even aspects of the self" (92). This is both a psychological and a sociological definition. Object relations understood as internalized symbolic meaning makes such a correlation possible. Weinstein and Platt argue that the three aspects of identification, internalization, and object loss form the psychoanalytic sociological basis for social change. The more significant aspect leading to change is that of object loss. Identification with and internalization of idealized objects can account for social stability. Change leads to the loss of the idealized aspects of the object identified with and internalized. This disappointment in the norms of behavior is identical to Durkheim's (1964) "anomie." "The inability of groups to translate internalized mandates into behavior as traditional and culturally sanctioned forms of behavior become—for whatever structural reason—unavailable, ineffective, or dysfunctional as a result of social change" (Weinstein and Platt 1973, 104). Thus the cultural context (including historical, social, and psychological events), which was necessary for the initiation of sacrifice, has to do with the disappointment of idealized cultural objects (object loss). Furthermore, the continuation of a ritual as a normative pattern of behavior would depend on the recurring object loss in the social and psychological lives of those who engage in the ritual. Or, if that is too bold a statement to make at this time, the identification with and internalization of idealized cultural objects, which perpetuate the emotional meaning of the ritual, is of a kind that "inhibits critical insight into one's social position (and thereby making one's social position tolerable)" (111–12).

Social change, including but not limited to liminal or marginal periods, creates the psychosocial context for sacrifice, and idealization, identification, and internalization maintain the efficacy of the ritual. The idealization of the cultural object is the idealization of cultural authority. The psychodynamics of object loss also hold the key for understanding the psychoanalytic sociological origin, meaning, and function of ritual sacrifice. The authority of sacrifice, using Weinstein and Platt's more generalized context, is due to idealization. This idealization establishes what Weinstein and Platt term a pregenital milieu, "a world of narcissistic entitlement, in which the 'bad' can be treated as brutally as anxiety and devotion to the 'good' require" (108). Such a narcissistic world would be open to ritual sacrifice, in which, again quoting Weinstein and Platt, "the difference between life and death is obscured and the 'removal of the source of tension' does not have the significance ordinarily associated with death" (108). Furthermore, as Weinstein and Platt remind, pregenital wishes are the origin for the capacity for violence as well as for the sacred. Of course they might be a bit annoyed at my quoting them slightly out of context. They are talking about authority in general. And yet, I contend that their general theory is completely applicable to a specific theory of sacrifice. What I do question about their theory is whether Erikson's ego psychology and its concept of identity are sufficient to account for the narcissistic disappointment in a cultural object embodied in a ritual that bleeds or cuts the life out of animal and human victims. Also, ego psychology is really unable to account for the issues raised in the anthropological analysis of sacrifice, notably the function of gender and patriliny.

Both Bakan and Jay argue that sacrifice, which functions within patrilineal descent, establishes and maintains male (fathers') predominance over female (mothers') in lineal descent. I have developed the thesis that men's efforts to control patrilineal descent is a correlative of the male-perceived power of women. In other words, the control of descent by and through men is a means of removing power from women and giving it to men. Such a process led Bakan to claim that "there is hardly a page in the Bible on which is not asserted in one way or another that the male can have children" (1968, 119). Douglas and Jay point out the relation between the power of women and the cultural (male) claim that such power is dangerous and polluting. Not only is the polluting power of childbirth (represented by the seeming contradiction of simultaneous life and blood) opposed to the purifying power of sacrifice (represented by death and blood), but sacrifice is a means of controlling the female power.

Power is one of the essential elements of a phenomenological definition of religion. Van der Leuuw, for example, begins his study of religion with several chapters on power. The first subject following that of power and the sacred is a chapter entitled "The Form of the Mother" (1938, 91–100). Van der Leuuw concludes the chapter by noting that "religions that are intensely oriented towards Will turn away from the mother and to the father" (100). That is, power, will, and salvation (from what?)—the subject of van der Leuuw's next chapter—moves from the mothers to the fathers, creating a dichotomy between the two realms. Sacrifice is a means of maintaining a continuum of dichotomous powers—separation of male and female (father and mother), purity and danger, clean and unclean, good and evil, culture and nature, and so on. But sacrifice also establishes the means of moving across these classificatory dichotomies for the purpose of acquiring the power from one side (e.g., the side represented by women, danger, pollution, evil, nature) for use by the other side (represented by men, safety, purity, good, culture). In other words, the male need to control women is related to the need to control the inexorable exigencies of nature as well. From a structural point of view, such logical movement is possible because of the human capacity to form, reform, and transform symbols (including symbolic classifications). As argued in the last chapter, the ability for symbol formation and transformation has its psychological foundation (dynamic and genetic) in the early years of each individual's life, and it includes a deep and significant relation between infant and mother (and later father, siblings, and culture). The effects of this infant-mother relation are longlasting and, as I also argued, powered in no small way by ambivalence and anxiety.

In his work on binary oppositions and its relation to sacrifice, Lévi-Strauss claims that the deep structure of binary systems is not equivalent to empirical reality. Yet, as Carol MacCormack notes, Lévi-Strauss "appeals to empirical 'reality' in constructing a model of human society in which women are simple passive objects of male activity" (1980, 11). Aside from the faulty anthropology Lévi-Strauss's position fosters, the problem for a psychological understanding of sacrifice is that it fails to take into consideration the psychological effect of women on men in the establishment and maintenance of symbolic action and symbolic systems. "Even within patrilinially organized societies [presumably including those that practice sacrifice]," continues MacCormack, "men ritually express anxiety about their dependence on women as regenerators of life" (14). Yet MacCormack barely ventures into this arena of male anxiety.

What is the dynamic and genetic basis for this anxiety? I have dismissed the drive theory of Freud for reasons shared by most anthropologists. And I have not been convinced by the psychobiological explanations of Jung, Klein, and Mahler. Each of these explanations contains elements that anticipate or parallel Kohut's psychology of narcissism. Yet Kohut's theory provides a more psychologically adequate explanation for the anxiety observed by anthropologists in their study of rituals and sacrifice. Clifford Geertz, for example, has moved behind the observation that sacrifice embodies conflict and contradiction and has tried to characterize the psychology of the anxiety of such conflict and contradiction by arguing that ritual helps create, express, and conceal the anxiety. To understand the psychology of ritual blood sacrifice, we also have had to move away from the classical drive theory, regardless of whether that theory emphasizes castration anxiety, separation anxiety, or moral anxiety. The male anxiety about women, which fuels the change from matriliny to patriliny (not simply from kinship to kingship, as Sagan argued) and which is embodied in ritual blood sacrifice, is anxiety about esteem, power, and differentiation. The anxiety is narcissistic. And narcissism fuels the religious symbols and rituals that address that anxiety.

Bakan also argues that there is a relationship between the psychological condition of separation/estrangement and sacrifice. This relationship has also been noted by Sagan, and I have already stated my objections to his use of Mahler's sociobiological observations of children (her theory of separation/individuation and separation anxiety) to provide a psychological explanation for that relationship. When we look at separation anxiety from the psychological point of view of narcissism, we find that the anxiety has less to do with the threat of object loss (what can be termed oedipal anxiety) and more to do with the threat of dedifferentiation (fragmentation and disintegration). The anxiety surrounding the breakdown of cultural (symbolic) boundaries is not drive anxiety. When cultural boundaries, distinctions, or classifications are affected by human development (babies becoming young boys, boys becoming men, first menses, death), by the breaking of taboos such as incest and adultery, or by any other seemingly unlimited set of transitional possibilities, both individual anxiety and social tension are obvious.

Likewise, the proclivity to classify is not fueled by psychobiological drives or anxiety about them, but by the psychological need to establish and maintain some semblance of order, i.e., "the cultural structure of a lifetime" (Kohut 1978, 2:822). For the anthropologist, the human being without these cultural patterns would be unfinished. In Geertz's terms such a person would be a formless monster. Human beings depend on symbolic systems to an extent "as to be decisive for his creatural viability and, as a result, his sensitivity to even the remotest indication that they may prove unable to cope with one or another aspect of experience raises within him the gravest sort of anxiety" (Geertz 1973, 99). For Geertz, chaos can threaten at three different points: at the limits of analytic capacities (metaphysical anxiety), at the limits of the power to endure (suffering—illness and mourning), and at the limits of moral insight (the problem of evil) (100–107). It is no accident that anxiety occurs at the limits of these human capacities. Limits are the place of liminality—the betwixt and between of Turner's anthropology of experience. Liminality is the place of the uncanny, the odd, the strange, the monstrous. It is the place of polluting danger and power, of *hama* and *buhonyi* (Douglas), and male prestige and *lek* (Geertz). It is also the place of mimetic desire (Girard) and separation anxiety (Sagan). What is the psychological means that relates all these elements under a psychology of narcissism and sacrifice? From most of the psychological theory we have reviewed, there is little disagreement that identification, idealization, and internalization provide the means of relation between the (developing) psychological apparatus and culture. How that occurs remains at the heart of the matter.

"Mourning," argues Homans, "is at the heart of the psychoanalytic view of religion and of religious healing" (1984, 135). I take this to mean that religion is a cultural and normative means of identifying and internalizing lost, de-idealized objects. In Part III I argue that the psychodynamic structure of sacrifice reflects a religious *inability* to mourn, to give up the idealized loss object through identification and internalization, because sacrifice reflects a psychodynamic tendency to acquire aspects of the idealized object that may not be internalized. Kohut's psychology of narcissism offers us a more advantageous (and therefore a bit more frightening) view of the processes that go into the development of a male narcissism embodied in what Homans terms the "farthest reaches of unconscious symbolic maneuvers" (149). Sacrifice certainly resides in such reaches.

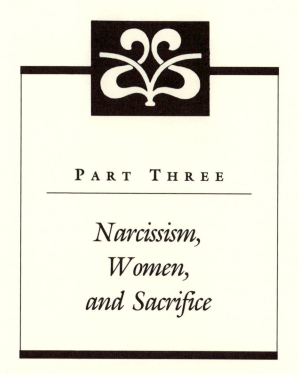

PART THREE

Narcissism,
Women,
and Sacrifice

ELEVEN

Self-Psychology, Narcissism, and Gender

The wicked people were gone, but fear remained. Fear always remains. A man may destroy everything within himself, love and hate and belief, even doubt; but as long as he clings to life he cannot destroy fear: the fear, subtle, indestructible, and terrible, that pervades his being; that tingles his thoughts; that lurks in his heart; that watches on his lips the struggle of his last breath. In his fear, the mild old Gobila offered extra human sacrifices to all the Evil Spirits that had taken possession of his white friends.

Joseph Conrad, *An Outpost of Progress*

A REVIEW OF Kohut's self-psychology and his theory of narcissism will, I hope, help answer the questions raised in the first two parts. His theory of the self-object and disintegration anxiety provides a useful means of understanding and explaining the relation between the formation and acquisition of symbols (via idealization, identification, and internalization), individual and group anxiety, and the near-universal occurrence of ritual blood sacrifice among patrilineal societies. The purpose of this chapter is to provide a summary of the significant elements of self-psychology: the self, self-objects—grandiose self, idealized parent imago, and twinship self-objects—disintegration anxiety, and narcissistic transferences—mirror, idealized, and twinship.

NARCISSISM, SELF-OBJECTS, AND THE SELF

EVEN THOUGH SIGNIFICANT fervor over his theoretical positions continues within the psychoanalytic community, Kohut's ideas and terminology have made their way into the theory and practice of psychoanalysis (Kohut 1978, 1:1–106). He spent almost thirty years formulating the psychoanalytic psychology of the self. Even his earliest writings reveal his interest in what he would later call narcissistic disintegration anxiety. In an early article on Thomas Mann's *Death in Venice*, Kohut wrote about the "disintegration of artistic sublimation" (1:107–30). In the article he makes two points that parallel the issues I have raised from both psychoanalytic and anthropological thought. The first, harmless and obvious enough, is that the author Mann's early childhood exhibits a strong degree of female influence (1:107). The second is about Mann's protagonist, Aschenbach. In describing the threat to Aschenbach's defensive system, Kohut writes: "Aschenbach's last dream is an expression of the breakdown of sublimation; it describes the destruction of 'the whole cultural structure of a lifetime'" (1:125): "the whole cultural structure of a lifetime" being quoted from Mann in the novel (Mann 1936, 430). Both statements are correlated through the sea-death-mother motif at the end of Aschenbach's life as he gazes at the boy Tadzio. Kohut remarks that the homosexual desire for the boy by the aging artist is an example of the psychological identification with the mother (the unsublimated object of desire).

In this article Kohut draws a psychological parallel between the artist and his creation. Aschenbach's "whole cultural structure of a lifetime" reflects the sublimated identification with his mother. The artist idealizes the boy Tadzio in the way his (Aschenbach's) mother should have idealized him (Aschenbach) as a child. Mann knows that the capacity to recreate an idealized image of the mother and the perfect image of the son through the sublimated symbolization eventually fails. All idealization ultimately fades and disappoints. In the case of Aschenbach, this activity to create a "cultural structure of a lifetime" in order to protect his fragile self from a dreaded and violent rage fails with age and illness. In a powerful dream, Aschenbach foresees the breakdown of that structure. The dream begins in dread: fear, disgust, and desire, with a shuddering of curiosity. Primitive sounds build until the dreamer hears a voice announcing what is to come. The dream vision is of a mountain similar to ones near the dreamer's home. Then from the trees he sees a whirling, growing band of men and animals come crashing toward him, overflowing down the side of the mountain, performing lascivious acts with one another. In a sense this dream represents the "monster" Geertz believes would exist were it not for the cultural structure of a lifetime. Mann believed identification with the mother ultimately leads to death, and eventually both Aschenbach and, presumably, Tadzio (Aschenbach's idealized image of himself as a perfect boy) die. Kohut observed that "in many of Mann's works the wish for the mother emerges as a longing for death." Yet what psychologically connects mother and death?

Almost thirty years later, Kohut returned to *Death in Venice*. By this time his theory of narcissism was more clearly defined and qualifies the oedipal themes and narcissistic function of sublimation Kohut believed operated within Aschenbach. Due to his ambivalent or ambiguous childhood environment, Aschenbach's childhood self remained in danger of fragmentation. Later in life he used his artistic creativity to provide himself with the experience of perfection and psychic structure (the experience of fundamental self-esteem). The works of art provided additions or replications of the self invested with narcissism, that is, perfection and power (idealization and omnipotence). *Death in Venice* is the story of the destruction of this ability. In the brief interlude between the decline in the creative ability to structure a perfect self and the final disintegration of the fragmenting childhood self, however, "we see the revival of the sexualized percussor of the artistic product: the beautiful boy (though frail and already marked for destruction) who is the symbolic stand-in for the core of the still unaltered childhood self which craves love and admiration" (Kohut 1978, 2:822).

For Kohut, this disintegration anxiety or fear of fragmentation became distinguishable from oedipal (separation, castration, or moral) anxiety during many psychoanalytic hours with patients who complained of vague fears of not being real or of their minds or bodies (the body-self) falling apart. Through the rediscovered Freudian insistence on introspection and empathy (vicarious introspection) as the correct mode of psychoanalytic observation and through the use of Freud's psycho-economic model (by the 1950s, the topological-structural model of the mind had become the model of choice among psychoanalysts), Kohut recognized in his patients psychodynamic elements that might not fit into a developmental theory with only one line of development.

By insisting on introspection and empathy, Kohut distanced himself from those efforts to combine other scientific theories with psychoanalytic theory. And because of this insistence, he sought to determine which of Freud's concepts were psychoanalytic and which were not. For example, when Freud hypothesized primary narcissism and primary masochism, he was doing so based first on the clinical observation of narcissism and masochism, and from that observation he supposed that they were the revival of developmentally earlier experiences. But when Freud further suggested that life and death instincts parallel the theory of primary narcissism and primary masochism, he then departed from the psychoanalytic mode of observation and theory. "The concepts of Eros and Thanatos," writes Kohut, "do not belong to a psychological theory grounded on the observational method of introspection and empathy but to a biological theory which must be based on different observational methods" (2:227).

Likewise, through introspection and empathy Kohut became aware that the kinds of psychoanalytic transferences that occurred while working with a patient who exhibited disintegration or fragmentation anxiety were qualitatively different from the neurotic transferences described in psychoanalytic literature. He noted that certain patients "used" him as though he were not an actual person, but a psychological vehicle to mirror aspects of themselves. He noticed also that when a patient idealized the analyst (either Kohut himself or the analyst Kohut was training) and the analyst resisted the idealization by introducing reality, the patient would react as though wounded.

Thus based on the clinical observation (introspection and empathy) of mirror and idealizing transferences, Kohut argued in 1966 for a second developmental line: narcissism (1:427–60). Kohut's theory of narcissism challenges Freud's theory of narcissism in two ways. First, Freud assumed that there is a single line of development, and narcissism is a stage along that line to full object love. Autoeroticism leads to narcissism, which leads to object love. Kohut, to the contrary, argued that the narcissistic line of development is independent of the instinctual drives of object libido. Second, Freud claimed that narcissism (particularly as it occurs within the analytic setting) is frustrated object libido recathected onto the ego. Kohut argued that not only is narcissism independent of object libido, but that many aspects of it are healthy and necessary for the development and continued well-being of every human being. Indeed, the very observational tools of psychoanalysis (introspection and empathy) are narcissistic transformations. In other words, narcissism is not something that people pass through or regress back to, it is the energy and form of what Kohut terms the self. Narcissism is always with us. To the charge that narcissism is more primitive and less healthy than object libido, Kohut believes "that these views do not stem primarily from an objective assessment of either the developmental position or adaptive value of narcissism, but are due to the improper intrusion of the altruistic value system of Western civilization" (1:427).

Along the independent line of narcissistic development, Kohut has theorized two transitional prestructures, which provide the primary psychological facilitation in the development of a self and of a sense of self and objects: the self-objects (Beers 1988). The psychological structuring of the self begins during the early childhood period of essentially undifferentiated, primary narcissism. Primary narcissism is the psychological experience of a perfect union of self and object. Primary narcissism begins to differentiate into self and object, the self eventually being transformed into an experience of subjective integrity separate from that of other objects (mother, father, animate and inanimate objects, etc.). This process of differentiation occurs as a result of unavoidable environmental frustrations. The developing psychological apparatus maintains the experience of perfection of primary narcissism through the establishment of two prestructural self-objects. The *"grandiose self"* enhances "a grandiose and exhibitionistic image of the self," while the previous perfection of primary narcissism is maintained by "an admired, omnipotent (transitional) self-object: the *idealized parent imago*" (Kohut 1971, 45).

Kohut first called the grandiose self the "narcissistic self," but because his whole theory was about narcissism and in order to be more descriptive, he changed the term to its present form (1978, 1:430). In Freud's terms the grandiose self corresponds to the "purified pleasure ego" (Freud 1915a, 135). The grandiose self refers to those characteristics that develop into a sense of self-esteem, the pleasure of being loved and admired, solipsistic tendencies, as well as self-satisfaction, achievement, and ambitions. Under optimal conditions the exhibitionism and grandiosity of the self become psychologically structured and integrated into a cohesive self along with the ego ideals internalized through the idealized parent imago.

Initially the idealized parent imago results from the psychological effort to maintain the blissful perfection of the undifferentiated experience in primary narcissism. The idealized parent imago refers to those characteristics that are internalized as the ego ideal, made possible through optimal frustration provided by the idealized self-object: "Every shortcoming detected in the idealized parent leads to a corresponding internal preservation of the externally lost quality of the object" (1978, 1:433). Or, put another way, "the ego ideal is that aspect of the superego which corresponds to the phase-specific, massive introjection of the idealized qualities of the object" (1:434).

Both the grandiose self and the idealized parent imago are enhanced and established through the child's relation to an empathically responding mirroring self-object, which finds its own joy in the child's idealizations of and merger with her/him. Thus, the child's experience of the mother or parent as a self-object needs to be mirrored and appreciated in order that the narcissistic transformations to ambitions and ideals take place. The nuclear self, as the result of the transformations of the two self-objects, "is not formed via conscious encouragement and praise and via conscious discouragement and rebuke, but by the deeply anchored responsiveness of the self-objects, which, in the last analysis, is a function of the self-objects' own nuclear selves" (1977, 100).

Kohut was convinced that psychoanalysis would move away from its emphasis on so-called primal events or traumata in a child's life and focus more and more on the facilitating factors that enhance or inhibit the formation and function of the early bipolar structures of the self. Furthermore, he came to believe "that the sense of abiding sameness along the time axis—a distinguishing attribute of the healthy self—is laid down early as the result of the abiding action-promoting tension gradient between the two major constituents of the nuclear self" (183). The nuclear self performs self-object functions throughout life. Kohut insisted on distinguishing between the activation of archaic self-objects and the use of mature self-objects (including cultural self-objects). Healthy narcissism reflects the use of self-objects to foster ambitions informed by ideals. Between the ambitions and ideals are the skills and talents used to maintain the tension gradient between the two self-objects. If the archaic self-objects have not been sufficiently internalized, they may be reactivated throughout life. In the next chapter, I argue that sacrifice reflects archaic self-object functions, not transformed narcissistic self-objects. For the present I review aspects of Kohut's theory that explain the results of failed narcissistic transformations.

NARCISSISTIC ANXIETY AND RAGE

WHEN THE INTERNALIZATION of the self-objects is not complete, parts of the grandiose self and the idealized parent imago remain split off from and inaccessible to the ego and its activities. With a traumatic loss of or disappointment in the idealized self-object, the internalization may not occur. That is, "the child does not acquire the needed internal structure, his psyche remains fixated on an archaic self-object, and the personality will throughout life be dependent on certain objects in what seems to be an intense form of object hunger" (1971, 45).

The hunger throughout life for idealized objects reflects the need to fill the void in a still-incomplete internal structure. Often the hunger is so intense that the incomplete ego ideal cannot contain the archaic forms of narcissism, and they will continue to intrude on later life. Such intrusions are experienced as anxiety. The anxiety or fear of narcissistic intrusion is the central anxiety of narcissistic disorders. Kohut claims this anxiety can take any of a number of forms:

> They are: fear of loss of the reality self through the ecstatic merger with the idealized parent imago, or through the quasi-religious regression toward a merger with God or with the universe; fear of loss of control with reality and fear of permanent isolation through the experience of unrealistic grandiosity; frightening experiences of shame and self-consciousness through the intrusion of exhibitionistic libido; and hypochondriacal worries about physical or mental illness due to hypocathexis of disconnected aspects of the body and the mind. (152)

The reality or nuclear self is the more or less cohesive self (which includes the experience of spatial boundaries and temporal cohesiveness). When the reality self is too incomplete (i.e., lacking in sufficient cohesion), it may be structurally too weak to withstand the powerful and intrusive hunger of the grandiose self for an idealized parent imago, which has not been introjected and internalized. The anxiety resulting from the dedifferentiating intrusion of the narcissistic prestructures leads to further ego activity to stem the tide of the narcissistic fragmentation of the self. The narcissistic hunger for merger and for exhibitionistic grandiosity, and the ego's anxiety about such activity, creates a high degree of ambivalence with regard to affect and an equally intense ambiguity with regard to activity.

The narcissistic hunger to merge with and be idealized by self-objects, and the fear of disintegration from such narcissistic intrusion, are two primary consequences of faulty empathic mirroring on the part of self-objects. There is another related psychological response to the faulty mirroring, which Kohut recognized in his treatment of narcissistic personality disorders and which most people also experience. Kohut called the faulty mirroring, which produces the intense narcissistic hunger or the fear of fragmentation, a narcissistic injury. (Freud had used the term "narcissistic injury to describe his grief reaction to the death of his daughter Sophie" [Bakan 1966, 156].) Narcissistic injuries, even when they occur in a well-structured nuclear self, are often experienced as narcissistic, shamefaced withdrawal or narcissistic rage. Narcissistic rage can occur as any number of feelings, ranging from slight disappointment or shame to extreme anger and aggression. Kohut's discussion of narcissistic rage is fundamental to a psychological understanding of sacrifice, because narcissistic shame and rage can lead to narcissistic violence and aggression. His discussion is also one of the places where Kohut ventures with any certainty out of the mind of the analysand and onto the plane of social behavior.

Disintegration and fragmentation fears are grounded in the psychological experience of the breakup of the body-self. Such a fragmentation can lead to the decathexis of certain parts of the body (i.e., fragments of the body-self). Once a fragment is no longer retained within the self it may be overstimulated in order to attempt a narcissistic recathexis. Persons with narcissistic disorders may use masturbation not so much as a sexual tension reliever but as a way to stimulate a feeling of power and aliveness. In cases of extreme psychosis, the fragment may be removed altogether. Self-mutilation can occur because the organ or part of the body the psychotic removes has lost its narcissistic connection with the rest of the body-self. For that reason it can be cut off and discarded (Kohut 1978, 2:633). Certain types of suicides are also narcissistically "based on the loss of libidinal cathexis of the self" (2:633). Both self-mutilations and suicides are accompanied by deep, albeit vague, feelings of emptiness, deadness, and/or shame.

Shame, however, may be accompanied not only by withdrawal (from the organ, life, or the social world); it may also lead to rage. When the shame is directed outwardly as narcissistic rage, it is accompanied by the "need for revenge, for righting a wrong, for undoing a hurt by whatever means, and a deeply anchored, unrelenting compulsion in the pursuit of all these aims, which gives no rest to those who have suffered a narcissistic injury" (2:638). Kohut argues that it is this deep, unrelenting compulsion for revenge that distinguishes this type of aggression from other types. To understand human aggression (and here perhaps his own narcissism keeps Kohut from stating that it is male aggression about which he is indeed talking), it has to be seen within the psychological context of narcissism and narcissistic rage. He sees the most dangerous aggression as being that connected with the bipolar constellation of narcissism: the grandiose self and the idealized parent imago. The most horrifying human violence occurs in those organized (I would add ritualized) actions in which the violence is fused with the belief in the actors' grandness and "their devotion to archaic omnipotent figures" (2:635). And Kohut argues that earlier considerations of aggression by Sigmund Freud and Anna Freud also need to be understood within the context of narcissism, shame, and rage, and not simply as a desire to change a passive act into an active one or a mechanism of identification. These factors should be understood within the broader context of shame and narcissistic injury. All these factors "help explain the readiness of the shame-prone individual to respond to a potentially shame-provoking situation by the employment of a simple remedy: the active (almost anticipatory) inflicting on others of those narcissistic injuries which he is most afraid of suffering himself" (2:638). Such aggression by the shame-prone individual is activated in the service of the archaic grandiose self that has not been integrated fully into a cohesive self. Such an individual does not perceive objects (other people) as independent centers of initiative. Rather he perceives their activity as wounds to his self, because they are narcissistic extensions of himself that he cannot control via the grandiose self. Likewise they do not correspond to the idealized self-object. In other words, "narcissistic rage arises when self or object fail to live up to the expectations directed at their [self-object] function" (2:644). The more weakly structured the self, the more it is prone to shame and rage, and the greater the need for a sense of control over an archaically experienced reality. Such a sense of control is essential "because the maintenance of self-esteem—and indeed of the self—depends upon the unconditional availability of the approving-mirroring selfobject or of the merger-permitting idealized one" (2:645).

NARCISSISTIC TRANSFERENCES

ALTHOUGH I HAVE discussed the origins and functions of the bipolar self-objects, I want to indicate their expression in relationships. Their discovery resulted from Kohut's observation of several forms of transference within the analytic setting, but Kohut realized that each kind of transference existed in the extra-analytic life of analysands.

The grandiose self finds expression through the mirror transference relationship. The more archaic form of the mirror transference is the merger of the self with the idealized parent imago. The less archaic form is the actual mirror transference in which the object is realistically separated from the self yet (as a self-object) participates in and confirms the self's narcissism (both the grandiosity and the idealizations). Mirror transferences have a tendency to reactivate infantile fantasies of grandiosity and exhibitionism. They can also foster more archaic merger fantasies.

In earlier writings Kohut included twinship or alter-ego transferences within the class of mirror transferences. Later he determined that twinship reflected a different psychological need. Mirror transferences reflect the life-long need to experience acceptance. Twinship transferences reflect the need to be like someone else. Writing about the clinical case on which he based this conclusion, Kohut noted: "her self was sustained by the presence of someone she knew was sufficiently like her to understand her and to be understood" (1984, 196). In this significant change in Kohut's theory, a woman provided the first opportunity to discover the difference between mirror and twinship transferences. Being like someone means imitating them, and in the desire to be like someone, a person acquires the imitated person's skills and talents, which are necessary to give expression to ambitions (via the grandiose self) and ideals (via the idealized parent imago).

The other form of transference occurs as a result of the reactivation of the idealized parent imago. In Kohut's theory the idealizing transference is an effort to regain the omnipotent feeling of narcissistic perfection "by assigning it to an archaic, rudimentary (transitional) self-object" (1971, 37). The idealized parent imago can be transferred onto a person or idea (such as God). Such reactivations may result from early disappointment in an idealized self-object or in a later oedipal object experienced as a threat (i.e., as diffuse narcissistic vulnerability, disintegration anxiety, or shame). The later recathexis of the idealized self-object is understood by Kohut to be a form of protection against the fragmentation of the self.

SELF-PSYCHOLOGY AND PSYCHOANALYTIC THEORY

SEVERAL FUNDAMENTAL ASPECTS of self-psychology distinguish Kohut's work from that of Klein, Winnicott, and Mahler. The primary difference lies in the mode of observation, which I discussed earlier in this chapter. Kohut's insistence on introspection and empathy (vicarious introspection) precludes the kinds of theoretical conclusions made by Klein and Mahler. Klein's analysis of children, for example, led her to theorize that verbalizable devouring and persecutory fantasies are present in early infancy. Kohut claimed that such a theory fails to use the correct empathic mode of observation and is in fact an example of adultomorphism. The same complaint can be made of Mahler's sociobiological observations. Instead of verbalizable fantasies of introjection (devouring) and projection (persecution), or infantile fears of separation, Kohut insisted on the economic (tension-reduction) model as the limit of observation (1977, 101).

In a review of *The Analysis of the Self*, Martin James (1973) saw in Kohut's theory of the self-object a similarity to Winnicott's theory of transitional objects and transitional phenomena. The similarity lessens, however, when we note that Winnicott is describing what he is observing, while Kohut is attempting to explain psychodynamics (the self-object transference) that occur in the analysis of adults who, in spite of defenses and resistances, are attempting to verbalize those psychodynamics. I do not believe this point can be overstated. Object relations theory (whether it be that of Klein, Winnicott, or Mahler) based on the observation of infants and children is extremely important, but it is not, strictly speaking, a psychoanalytic explanation. This is not to say that object relations theory has no place in psychoanalysis. Far from it. I am only arguing here that the self-object has more psychological structure and application for gender studies than Winnicott's transitional object.

A similar criticism can be made of Erikson's term *identity* used by Weinstein and Platt. Identity is a descriptive term that, from a psychoanalytic point of view, has more to do with conscious and preconscious configurations, as contrasted with the self-object configurations of prestructural psychic activity. Kohut distinguished *self* and *identity* in a letter he wrote in 1975, in which he argued that the self is a "depth-psychological concept and refers to the core of the personality made up of various constituents in the interplay with the child's earliest self-objects" (1978, 1:471–72 n. 1). Identity refers to the relation between the already developed self and the sociocultural roles of the individual.

Critics of Kohut's position have tended to focus more on his introduction of the self-objects and the independent line of narcissistic development. Thus, they can compare his work to this theory or that theory. Kohut readily admits that metapsychological terms (e.g., self-object, grandiose self, idealized parent imago) are psychoanalytic tools useful in the interpretation and explanation of psychodynamic activity. But the emphasis Kohut prefers is on the *mode of observation* (which, he insists, is very much in the tradition of Freud's psychoanalytic work), rather than on the particular metapsychological nomenclature used.

NARCISSISM AND GENDER: KOHUTIAN EMPATHY AT ITS LIMITS

IF I TAKE Kohut's position seriously—that introspection and empathy constitute the correct mode of psychoanalytic observation—then I need to account for the relation between that mode of observation and the particular clinical cases he and his colleagues present as evidence of specific aspects of self-psychology. In reviewing the twenty-four cases presented in the main self-psychology texts, one observation that can be made is that a majority of cases are men (eighteen, compared to six women). *The Analysis of the Self* contains cases A-Q (seventeen cases: fifteen men, two women); *The Restoration of the Self* contains cases A, C-F, I, J, M and adds U-Y (five additional cases: three men, two women); *The Psychology of the Self* contains cases B, I, M, E and adds R and Mrs. Apple (two cases, both women); Kernberg (1975) presents seven cases (five men, two women). With such a discrepancy between the number of men and women, I had expected some discussion of the relation between gender and narcissism, yet in the texts I examined, "gender" was not an entry in any index and beyond some brief discussions of gender identity, I could find no concern with gender. However, in a discussion of "gender identity," Kohut writes against postulating gender identity in early life, arguing instead for "activity or passivity as precursors of masculinity or femininity" (1978, 2:784–85 n. 1). The high ratio of men to women is all the more puzzling when considered with the fact that fully two-thirds of all psychiatric patients in America are women (Philipson 1985, 215). Such a disproportionate number of men to women in the case material of self-psychology leads Ilene Philipson to conclude that "narcissism—as a personality type and pathological disorder—denotes a way of being in the world that is primarily if not exclusively experienced by men" (215). Her assertion has merit, and I want to examine the reasons for her conclusion.

After reviewing theories of the narcissistic period of development (the process of separating from the mother and establishing the self as a subjective center of initiative), Philipson argues that the process is different for boys and girls because of the character of the empathic mirroring (Kohut) or "holding environment" (Winnicott) that the mother provides the infant: "While mothers may see and tend to their sons and daughters on the basis of feelings they have toward themselves and other significant figures, rather than on the basis of their children's own expressed needs, they are more likely to view sons as *others* or *objects* in their unconscious (and . . . not so unconscious) mental life, and daughters as extensions of themselves" (221–22). The self-psychological apparatus (to a great extent related to and reflecting the quality of the maternal self-object) in men and women is going to be different, particularly in the area of the defenses constructed to ward off unempathic self-object intrusions and esteem depletion. Because women are reared by women, "they develop [more fluid] ego boundaries that allow or compel them to feel esteemed and loved through identification or 'fusion' with others" (225). They compensate for the depletion in self-esteem by operating as continuations or extensions of others. When Kohut revised his theory to distinguish a twinship self-object experience (the experience of essential alikeness or essential identification) from that of a mirroring self-object experience, the example he presented was of a woman analysand (1984, 194–95).

Because their maternal self-objects have fostered more rigid ego boundaries, men "are more likely to display feelings of grandiosity and extreme self-centeredness, and to need the admiration of others" (Philipson 1985, 225). Both men and women are *re-enacting* the experience of the maternal self-object: men as the other object of the mother, women as the subjective extension of the mother. Philipson goes on to complain that the "characteristically female attempt to gain self valuation through merger with the mother and mother-substitutes is neglected by Kohut, Kernberg, and Lasch" (225). She adds that the term *narcissism* needs to be redefined to include women's experience.

Philipson's claims are well made. In my review of Kohut, there is a lack of concern for gender issues. Yet numbers alone are not sufficient proof that Kohut has reached faulty clinical conclusions in those cases involving women clients. Nor are the conclusions about one gender sufficient grounds for the exclusion of the other gender. And Philipson acknowledges that "the low esteem, the deficient psychic structure, and the deeply unconscious hunger for love that is at the root of the narcissistic dilemma is shared by both women and men" (225). Nevertheless, her assertion may indeed be correct that women tend to overcome narcissistic impoverishments through identification and merger with maternal self-objects and that men tend to do so through grandiose exhibitionism reflecting the need to be admired by the self-objects. It seems reasonable to believe that the difference has to do with the gender-specific forms of empathic response by the maternal self-object during the pre-structural and early narcissistic period of development. Philipson's analysis helps account for the reaction to faulty mirroring (narcissistic injury), which, at least in the clinical cases provided by self-psychology, leads to a preponderance of narcissistic hunger in women (the need to merge) and of narcissistic grandiosity, rage, sadistic fantasies, and violence in men (the need to control and be admired).

This evidence also helps in understanding the psychological origins of why men *and* women fear women (the omnipotent self-object) but why primarily *men* need to control women. Females can identify with that omnipotent self-object, while males identify with it but also have to separate from it at the same time. Yet the maternal self-object remains a powerful configuration within the ambivalent male self. If its power cannot be finally acquired through identification, it has to be acquired through other means.

TWELVE

Male Narcissism, Women, and Sacrifice

FROM AN ANTHROPOLOGICAL point of view, the cultural context of sacrifice includes the conflicts and contradictions that arise both naturally (logically) or deliberately out of symbolic classificatory systems. These systems are constructed around a sacred order that reflects and protects the inclusive structures of social reality. The historical foundation of social reality is the kinship system. Like most classificatory systems, kinship systems are based on binary oppositions. The kinship surrounding the vast majority of sacrificial systems is patriliny. The binary opposition of the patrilineal kinship system is based on a father/mother, male/female dichotomy.

In qualifying Lévi-Strauss's claim that the mind innately classifies reality through binary oppositions, I have argued that binary or bipolar constructions of reality have their psychological origins in the early narcissistic period of life. MacCormack notes that "the first distinction all new-born humans make is that between self and nurturing other" (1980, 2–3). She goes on to ask, "What is the exact relationship between the organizing work of the unconscious and the conceptual domain of social structure, political relations, and so forth?" (3). Any answer to that question requires a developmental model of the mind.

Through the review of anthropological and dynamic psychological theory in Parts I and II, I developed the thesis that ritual blood sacrifice embodies male and male-identified anxiety and men's symbolic efforts to control and acquire the experienced power of women. In this chapter I want to present a gender-specific psychoanalytic theory of sacrifice using Kohut's model of the mind. One ad-

137

vantage to Kohut's psychology of the self for anthropology is that it diminishes the bothersome nature/nurture argument. The question of whether nature or culture is the basis for this or that human characteristic becomes irrelevant, because without adequate empathic and mirroring self-objects, humans never develop the psychological structure necessary to internalize the social and cultural world. As noted earlier, Mary Douglas wrote that "the only one who holds nothing sacred is the one who has not internalised the norms of any community" (1975, xv). Geertz (1973) says as much when he asserts that without the symbolic systems mediated to the developing psychological apparatus through the parent(s), a human being would remain a formless monster. From a psychoanalytic point of view, this means that parental self-objects begin to provide normative structure for transforming the grandiose self and idealized parent imago into socially realistic ambitions and ideals, mediated by individual talents and skills.

The formation of the bipolar self through the grandiose and idealized self-objects can, even under optimal conditions, become fraught with anxiety, which can be experienced throughout life. The anxiety centers around esteem issues and is marked by intense hunger for the idealized self-object. It is also marked by disintegration anxiety (the fear of fragmentation of the grandiose self). Because the maternal self-object (the idealized parent imago) provides the initial ideals and mirroring for the developing psychological apparatus, subsequent identification and internalization necessary for the continued socialization of an individual is built on this original bipolar structure, and the boundaries of the self continue to be narcissistically related to the internalized social structure.

If, as I have been arguing, gender plays an important part in the self-structuring of male and female psychological apparatuses, men will be more likely to feel threatened by factors affecting their grandiose sense of self-esteem, prestige, and power because they have experienced the omnipotent maternal self-object as Other, rather than experiencing themselves as subjective extensions of the self-object, as will be the case with women. Likewise, they are unable throughout life to ever fully identify with that self-object as woman the way that women can. And, as Philipson (1985) notes, because women have more fluid ego boundaries, they are less likely to feel overly anxious or threatened by marginality—the states of ambiguity that exist amidst all social structures. Indeed, women (and their children) are themselves the primary marginal people in a patrilineal society.

For men, periods of marginality threaten their more rigid ego boundaries. I believe this is true for several related reasons. The male sense of self is based on the maintenance of distinctions. René Girard went so far as to claim that distinctions maintain peace while the loss of distinctions leads to rivalry and violence. This need for distinctions has its origins in the self/self-object period of early narcissism, when the male psychological apparatus is distinguishing from the maternal self-object and structuring the self. Marginality is an intrusion into a social structure that reflects and maintains the structure of the self. A male-determined, patrilineal social structure confronted with marginality (e.g., sacred pollution) is equivalent to an individual man experiencing a narcissistic intrusion of an archaic (maternal) self-object. Indeed, from the point of view of the self-object function, the two are indistinguishable.

I need to say something more about the narcissistic anxiety arising during structural marginality. Anxiety is the psychological place where men and women most differ with regards to marginality. Because of the gender-specific quality of the maternal self-object's empathic mirroring, when confronted with marginality, women are more likely to identify with the marginality. They have the compensatory structures that allow for merger and equilibrium (a kind of "I am not helpless because I am connected"). Men, on the other hand, will respond to marginality in a different way, via the activation of the grandiose self ("I am not helpless because I am the most powerful"). Geertz clearly shows how that grandiosity works in the Balinese cockfights. Although Kohut uses the term *fear*, marginal anxiety is much more than fear. In truth, anxiety lacks the object that fear has. I prefer the term *dread* to describe the narcissistic experience of marginality. With dread there is both desire and disgust. The ambiguity of distinctions, which marginality offers, creates both the desire for and disgust of merger, as well as the desire for and disgust of the self as separate. The dread of margins is, in fact, desire and disgust on both sides of the ambiguous boundary.

Kierkegaard (1946) was the first modern thinker to articulate the dual side of narcissistic (he termed it *aesthetic*) dread, and his analysis is psychoanalytically correct. On the one side, dread has no object. In fact, dread is the destruction of subject and object. And on the other side, dread is the possibility of the self being constituted (in Kohut's terms, through the transmuting internalization of the self-objects). Kierkegaard's discussion of the aesthetic stage and the concept of dread are remarkably parallel to many of Kohut's discussions of narcissistic personality disorders. Marginal anxiety, then, is the place where the self either transforms the self-objects (via identification and internalization) or is fragmented by them.

As I have indicated, on the one hand, women appear more able to identify with and internalize marginal states. Communitas is one result of marginal anxiety, and it is perhaps psychologically more available to women. I really do not want to say much more about women; they can write their own psychologies. On the other hand, the psychological apparatus of men experiences sacred pollution or transitional intrusions as threats of self-disintegration. These threats are self-object wounds, and they can lead to rage and to the possibility of aggression and violence. Unlike the idealized mother imago of the narcissistic period, the cultural self-object experience cannot adequately mirror male grandiosity. Consequently, male identification with the now-transformed omnipotent (albeit maternal idealized) self-object remains incomplete. This, I believe, is why men envy and fear women, why they attempt to control and degrade them, and why sacrifice is the male ritual of choice. I am suggesting that male narcissistic self-objects are embodied in the symbols of a culture. I am further suggesting that religious rituals embody and hide these male narcissistic self-objects. And the symbol that ties the male narcissistic need for, resentment of, and envy of the omnipotent maternal self-object (and the women who represent it to men) is the blood sacrifice.

THE SELF-OBJECT AND THE SYMBOL OF SACRIFICE

BECAUSE THE MARGINALITY desired and feared by men has a strong connection to narcissism, in a self-psychological understanding, sacrifice (the symbolic act that responds to marginality) is comprised of four interrelated narcissistic self-object functions. Through these self-object functions, sacrifice can express: (1) the grandiose desire for merger with an idealized self-object; (2) the dread of such a merger through the act of separation (de-identification, differentiation, expiation, prophylaxis); (3) the narcissistic rage and violence surrounding the disappointment in the merger with and separation from the self-object; and, (4) the symbolic transfer and transformation of omnipotence from the idealized maternal self-object to the grandiose male self.

Sacrifice as Merger

ACCORDING TO LÉVI-STRAUSS, Douglas, and Turner, sacrifice functions to bring two symbolic orders or domains into the same symbolic proximity. Even if the merger of the two orders only occurs at the instant of the immolation, two orders are joined. This merger of orders in the marginal space has a narcissistic element. A narcissistic merger, identical to a symbolic merger, is one in which differences become more vague. The distinction between the sacred and the profane, like the distinction between the self and the mirroring or merged self-object, is reduced. Classifications break down. Self and object become more connected by becoming less distinct.

When the self-object function of sacrifice occurs in this way, narcissistic merger is not unlike Turner's concept of communitas. Communitas is the experience of unstructured, undifferentiated homogeneity. The significant difference between narcissism and communitas is that Turner understands communitas as the recognition by the participants of equality and human bonds, while the self-objects of narcissism are prestructural, prelinguistic, and thus precognitive. There can be no recognition in a precognitive apparatus. The recognition of communitas is a later development, which contains the energy and form of the earlier, now transformed, narcissistic prestructures. Communitas has to do with understanding sacrifice; narcissism with explaining it. It would be more correct to say that communitas and empathy are equivalent concepts stemming from and containing narcissistic elements expressing the desire to be connected or even merged.

Men sacrifice in order to be connected with their idealized and omnipotent self-objects. The need to merge with the idealized self-object is the most (psychologically) primitive activation of the grandiose self. That activation is, as noted, recognizable in the mirror transference, "in which the child attempts to save the originally all-embracing narcissism by concentrating perfection and power upon the self—here called the grandiose self—and by turning away disdainfully from an outside in which all imperfections have been assigned" (Kohut 1971, 106). When sacrifice serves to merge the domain of the divine with that of the human (the sacred with the profane, the clean with the polluted), the self-object function is to merge the self with the omnipotent self-object. That is the most archaic form of the sacrifice as merger. Or, if the function is less archaic, the sacrifice attempts to acquire the power of that (maternal) self-object by bringing the two domains into close proximity so that through the victim the power can be transferred from the divine to the human. In this case the men who sacrifice are hoping there is enough similarity (twinship) between the two domains that the transfer is possible..

The least archaic self-object function of the sacrifice as merger is to simply have the omnipotent self-object mirror the power (the need for power) of the men who sacrifice. Under this function would fall the need for power and control in the face of suffering, death, or other unavoidable disappointments. A function such as this led Masud Khan to conclude that "it is precisely this need in the human individual for his or her psychic pain to be witnessed silently and unobtrusively by *the other*, that led to the creation of the omni-presence of God in human lives" (1981, 414).

Sacrifice as Separation

PERIODS OF MARGINALITY, like the potential for narcissistic merger, increase the likelihood of narcissistic anxiety. Psychoanalytically, the self fears its own dedifferentiating fragmentation, its own destruction (which is also the central anxiety in Jung's theory of sacrifice). This fear can be expressed as the fear of the loss of power, control, autonomy, and/or meaning. To merge is to lose the self by becoming nothing again in the original narcissistic state. There is a danger in getting too close to the idealized self-object, because of the potential for the breakup of the self.

Anthropologists argue that the binary classification of social reality is an innate and universal activity. Such an assertion helps us understand and describe the danger of classification (based on patriliny in the case of sacrifice) breakdowns and margin mergers. As I claimed above, the breakdown of classifications of symbolic structures is felt as a real threat because the created structures of idealized identification are intended to guard against narcissistic fragmentation. Here I am simply adding a self-psychological explanation to Durkheim's theory of the role played by identification, sentiment, and anomie in classificatory systems.

The primal classification, occurring during the narcissistic period of the development of the bipolar self and upon which all subsequent classifications depend (both created and learned), is the classification ultimately threatened by undifferentiated, liminal, and narcissistic merger. I am arguing that anxiety resulting from the breakdown of classifications stems from a prestructural narcissistic stage of development. The cultural relativity of classification systems indicates that the content is not the causative source of anxiety. In other words, anxiety is not simply a learned reaction. The fact that any number of diverse classification breakdowns can give rise to similar states of anxiety suggests that this anxiety is a response to *prestructural* elements, which, through a process of transmuting internalization, creates and fuels the social classificatory structures.

Again, because men have more rigid self boundaries, dedifferentiation or disintegration anxiety leads to a very strong need to differentiate or separate. The sacrifice that serves this self-object function is that of expiation. In this case, the intrusive idealized self-object, which leads to the fragmentation anxiety, is experienced as a dangerous pollution causing the sin, sickness, death, or other change in the classificatory system. The need to maintain separation leads to a split in the social body, as Douglas claims. The sacrifice then functions as a means of splitting off 'not-me' parts from idealized reality and placing them outside of the narcissistically fueled classificatory system.

The anxiety (narcissistic dread) surrounding the marginal period is, as I have noted before, fueled by both desire and disgust. In expiation sacrifice, that which evokes disgust (the threat of fragmentation by the intrusive idealized self-object) is classified as 'not-me' and is symbolically embodied in a surrogate or substitute victim, which is killed or scapegoated. Psychologically, the self-object is split into good and bad parts in order to maintain the idealized classifications of reality. Because men presumably classify reality, the split-off parts almost invariably include those experiences having to do with women, sex, and childbirth.

Sacrifice as Narcissistic Rage and Violence

HUBERT AND MAUSS were amazed by the "remarkable fact that, in a general way, sacrifice could serve two such contradictory aims as that of inducing a state of sanctity and that of dispelling a state of sin" (1964, 58). I believe the two self-objects of the bipolar self help explain how such a contradiction (in Turner's terms, both prophylaxis *and* abandonment) is psychologically possible and how some sacrifices can be either conjunctive or disjunctive or both. Because sacrifice is psychologically an embodiment of self-object functions, the longed-for merger cannot actually take place. Likewise, the separation can never be absolute. Rather, hunger for merger and the desire for rigid ego boundaries reflect the ambivalent tension gradient between the two self-objects. The need to merge is fueled by the longing for the omnipotence of the maternal self-object and for that self-object to mirror the omnipotence of the grandiose self, while the need to remain separate reflects the fear of the intrusive power of the same maternal self-object.

I want to look more closely at the psychology of failed identification/merger and failed idealization/separation. Because male narcissistic identification with the maternal self-object is less likely to receive confirming mirroring from the self-object, the grandiose parts of the self experience the failed identification as a narcissistic injury. Narcissistic injury can lead to narcissistic rage and even aggression. The violence of sacrifice, then, is also a socially transformed expression of the rage resulting from the failed identification with the omnipotence of the idealized self-object. That is part of the answer to the question of the violence of sacrifice. While maternal self-object identification may not receive adequate empathic confirmation, however, later identifications with paternal and other male self-objects are likely to succeed. And what is internalized through male self-objects includes the male self-objects' own internalized experience of failed identification with maternal self-objects.

The internalization of male self-objects also includes other aspects of male identification. Some identifications may reflect psychobiological or cultural vestiges of earlier human evolution. For example, the violent relation between a sacrificial animal and men may have a strong correlation either to the human control over animals that were domesticated and/or to the significance of hunting animals in human evolution. By mentioning this, however, I am not proposing an innate proclivity for male violence. Sacrifice is not simply a cultural way to give men a safe way to kill, although it is that, because of some evolutionary proclivity for violence. I am suggesting that the complex ritual violence performed by men is an ancient way for men to identify with each other as men, and to separate from women. As one anthropologist notes: "In both violent and aggressive action male bonding is the predominant instrument of organization" (Tiger 1969, 171).

In addition to being a function of violence, male bonding is also a cause of violence. This causal relation results from narcissistic identification within the male bond group and separation from the non-male group (i.e., women, children, slaves, captives, and other marginal people, creatures, and self-objects). The split between 'me' and 'not-me,' between group and not-group, reflects the tension between the grandiose self and the threatened fragmentation of the self by the split-off, bad aspects of the idealized self-object (the term *bad* is a judgment that can only rightly be applied after speech is structured; i.e., the original self-objects are pre-structural and therefore neither bad nor good). The group, therefore, is going to perceive outsiders as threats or sources of danger because outsiders affect the narcissistic equilibrium of the group. Outsiders intrude on the boundaries of the group's collective identification (its grandiose self and ideals). Wounds lead to rage and potential violence, as any urban street gang's behavior shows. The sacrificial victim, then, is a marginal being on which is focused the 'not-me' (narcissistically split-off) parts, which are then destroyed or violently cut off from the group's culture. This psychological process is identical to Bakan's "idea of sacrifice in which that which is 'me' is made into something 'not-me,' and in which that 'not-me' is sacrificed in order that 'I' might continue to live" (1968, 79). In the violent response to an intruder, the narcissistic identification with that intruder is apparent because the violence reflects, in Kohut's terms, "the active (almost anticipatory) inflicting on others of those narcissistic injuries which he is most afraid of suffering himself" (1978, 2:638).

Sacrifice as the Transfer of Omnipotence from the Maternal to the Male

WHEN MEN BOND, they gain self-validation and self-affirmation through a shared, idealized male self-object. The bonding to older men by boys and younger men gives all (young and old) self-respect, confidence, and skills they desire, but it also further separates the men from their maternal self-objects. This is clearly the case in many secret male societies in which initiation rites often imitate the role of women in childbirth. One social scientist has suggested that these ceremonies "appear to express an envy of the female role. For example, the initiation is often culturally perceived as a rebirth ritual in which men take a child and bring about his birth as a man by magical techniques stolen long ago from women" (D'Andrade 1958, 196). The role of gender envy has also been discussed by Bruno Bettelheim (1955). Envy indicates that while male bonding attempts to separate the men from the women, the separation conceals a male desire for identification with and acquisition of the power of the maternal self-object. Initiation rites indicate this ambivalence and narcissistic ambiguity. D'Andrade continues: "The need for the initiate to prove his manhood by bearing extreme fatigue and pain [as though in birthing labor and childbirth] appears to indicate some uncertainty in sex identity" (196).

Sacrifice, as Jay (1985) argues, takes away the power and value of descent from the mother and ritually gives it to the father. Male dimorphic dominance, bonding, and the exclusion of women from the center of power are confirmed by sacrifice. The "magical techniques" of women were "stolen" because they were experienced by men as powerful, as dangerous, as intrusive. Men envy the perceived power of women and create ritual actions of blood and rebirth in order to have equivalent power and control over life and death. But Jay's position lacks a male psychology to explain the male perception of women's power. This psychological aspect of sacrifice reflects its twinship self-object function. The transfer of "magical techniques" is the acquisition of skills and talents based on identification and alikeness.

CONCLUSION

IN THIS CHAPTER, I have attempted an explanation that does not contradict an anthropological understanding of sacrifice or the self-psychological explanation of narcissism and the male self. I have also fleshed out the psychological part of a theory in which men sacrifice in order to move closer to, gain distance from, or acquire the experience of power and perfection. The ritual reenacts the terror of merger and separation, which men experience as the tension gradient between the grandiose self and the idealized maternal self-object during the early period of narcissism. This idealized reenactment gives men power (from their point of view, the power is made available to them or they receive the effects of it), which was originally located in the experience of the maternal self-object. The cultural function and result of this transfer of power is that women are excluded from exercising cultural power (unless kinship lineage allows one to rule as queen, etc., while the rest are ruled by men—fathers, husbands, and in matrilineal societies, brothers and sons). The need to sacrifice occurs when the male narcissistically invested social structures have their boundaries tested or threatened, that is, whenever self-objects intrude. The psychology of narcissism developed by Heinz Kohut has helped me take several different interpretations and explanations of sacrifice and place them within a context that clarifies, relates, and supports them. This theory seems to make sense. But the proof of a theory lies in its usefulness for explaining actual human affect and behavior, the task of the next two chapters.

THIRTEEN

Malekula: Pigs, Women, and Sacrifice

IN THIS CHAPTER the self-psychological theory of sacrifice I have developed is applied to an analysis of pig sacrifices found on Malekula, an island of Vanuatu (formerly New Hebrides) in the Melanesian archipelagoes, about nine hundred miles from the northwest coast of Australia. The description of Malekula and its surrounding islands, particularly Vao, is taken from the extensive ethnographic work done by John Layard (1942), to a lesser extent that of Thomas Harrison (1939) and A. B. Deacon (1934). I have organized the descriptive material under three subheadings: social context, mythology, and rites.

SOCIAL CONTEXT

"ALL MELANESIAN SOCIETIES," according to Lawrence and Meggitt, "are the same general type. All are stateless and lack central authority. [And] all stress kinship and descent in the formation of important local groupings" (1965, 5). While the peoples of the Highlands of New Guinea are exclusively patrilineal in their descent systems, those of the other islands exhibit both patrilineal and matrilineal descent organizations, as well as other related variations.

The idea of "religion" apart from the very fabric of a person and society was unknown to the peoples of Melanesia before the introduction of Christianity. Their indigenous beliefs and rituals, however, seem to be representative of a genus common to all. They believe in spirit-beings, occult forces, and totems with which they can communicate in order to affect the physical and moral conditions surrounding the people. Among the most important functions of spirit-beings is the guardianship of the dead.

The social life of each Melanesian society is dominated by male graded societies, parts of which are kept secret from children and women—although most women know the secrets. Initiation into the male society almost always involves the shedding of the initiates' blood—through nose bleeding, penile incision, and beating until the skin bleeds. The male cult of the graded society has economic and political ends. It controls reproduction and descent, and it provides access to the world of the dead. Related to this is perhaps the best-known aspect of Melanesian life common to most societies: the pervasive separation of and antagonism (if not open hostility) between the sexes (Meigs 1984; Gelber 1986; Strathern 1988; Lidz and Lidz 1989).

Pigs play a pivotal symbolic role in the total life of many Malekulan societies. Funabiki humorously characterizes the predominance of pigs in social life, conversation, and ritual scenes among the south Malekulan society of Mbotgote as a "pig complex" (1981, 173). Jolly (1981) contends that men in south Pentecost appropriate pigs ideologically by identifying with them. Through pigs a man acquires prestige and rank; he acquires wives; he acquires a soul necessary for the journey to the dead. Through pigs a man can communicate with the spirit-beings—his ancestors, the cultural heroes and deities, as well as the tricksters, demons, pucks, and other non-empirical powers, which are very close to the physical world and which can affect practically anything.

In Layard's opinion the cultural element that most affected and determined the social structure and life on the island was the kinship system—especially the regulations of marriage and descent—and the megalithic rituals surrounding the lifelong initiation of the men into and through the graded society. The entire system or cycle of rites and sacrifices is called the Maki. When Layard did his study, the islands throughout New Hebrides were undergoing many serious social and cultural changes, not the least of which was, in Layard's view, an apparent changeover from a system of matrilineal descent to that of patrilineal descent. The consequences of duel systems operating simultaneously could be seen in the number of wars fought over the issue of marriage and kinship. The problems encompassing the kinship system so impressed Layard that he gives it the central position for understanding the Maki rites. The more deeply he studied the myths and rituals of Malekula, the more he was convinced that their development was based on the problems of the kinship system (1942, 23).

Evidently the ideological causes of the conflicts surrounding marriage and kinship anomalies occur because the rules that apply to either a matrilineal or a patrilineal system are confused when both systems are simultaneously operating. For example, previously under a matrilineal system a man (EGO) could marry his mother's brother's widow (MBW). In the patrilineal system, the MBW does not belong to the same moiety as the EGO and since the EGO-MBW now can occur, there is a breakdown in social structure (class). This is important in a patrilocal graded society for which lineage is essential in the establishment of class, because the patrilocal side of the society sacrifices pigs through the matrilineal side in order to move up the graded society (*see* Patterson 1981). Although Layard is uncertain how the transition from matrilineal to patrilineal descent was occurring, the result was that such organizational changes affected the structure of the villages. Each village was bisected into two sub-villages. Every double-village was made up of two matrilineal moieties existing and modified by an overt patrilocal social organization. The significance of these changes in the kinship system can be seen in what both the people and Layard claim as the chief causes of war: kinship and marriage violations. According to Layard's informants "the fighting accompanying the new regime [leading to the what Layard believed to be a changeover from matrilineal to patrilineal descent] was so bitter that the people of Vao now put down all warfare to this occurrence" (1942, 165).

Parallel with and reflective of the kinship system and its conflicts is the graded society. Through the successive acquisition of higher social ranks a man obtains a soul. Souls are crucial for men, because only with a soul does a man have any chance of withstanding annihilation after death. Indeed, Layard thinks that the graded society is "in one of its aspects, an actual representation of the journey of the dead" (220). In order to explore this idea further, I want to examine three relevant mythologies that will help validate Layard's claim.

MYTHOLOGY

The Story of To-wewe and the Origin of the Maki Rites

IN THIS MYTH To-wewe, an eldest son, marries his full sister. The two gather one hundred kernels of the *tawo* tree and intend to perform the Maki sacrifice. They sing a song in which they lament the amount of fighting that occurs on the islands around them. After the song they prepare to "sacrifice" the kernels, but their father intercedes and substitutes a tusked boar. He tells his son to sacrifice; he forbids his daughter from the same. Subsequent to this first sacrifice, nine more sons are born to the father. In his desire to test their loyalty to him, the father solicits the aid of his wife. He orders her to surreptitiously expose her genitals to each of the sons. Whichever ones avert their eyes and leave are "good," but the ones who see and want to copulate are "bad." Only To-wewe "did wrong" with her, and she returns to her husband carrying the broken yam (the sign of the desire for incest). He tells To-wewe that his eldest (*beteram*) has done wrong and he will have no further dealings with him.

The original sacrifice performed by To-wewe was called *Ramben*, which is also the name of the first part of the Maki rite. The father goes on to teach the sons the second part, known as *Maki Ru* (High Maki). While he sends To-wewe back to the house on an errand, he has the other nine brothers perform the sacrifices. To-wewe returns furious, and the father tries to soothe him by promising to allow To-wewe at a later time to perform the rite. But To-wewe takes the circle-tusked boar he had intended to sacrifice and places it in the hollow trunk of a *nev* tree. Then, singing the same song he and his sister-wife had sung over the *tawo* kernels, he places himself in the hollow trunk and dies (286). A circle-tusked boar is one in which the large lower rooting tusks have been allowed to grow out of the jaw and circling back re-entering the jaw and then reappearing a second time, thus forming a circle. This occurs as a result of the upper teeth, which normally grind against the tusks, being knocked out, thereby allowing the tusk to grow unimpeded in its circular fashion (*see* Funabiki 1981, 177). Circle-tuskers are the most valued of all pigs.

The myth seems to suggest that one of the functions of the Maki is to put a stop to war. Layard confirms this elsewhere when he remarks that "the Maki itself . . . is held by the natives to constitute the main force in their culture making for peace" (1942, 15). If the chief cause of war results from marriage and kinship disputes, then the Maki, by stopping the fighting, must somehow also be putting a stop to kinship disputes or even their causes.

We also see in the myth that the first sacrifice by a brother and sister is refused, and women are excluded from performing the rite.

In the second part of the myth, the death of the doubly incestuous son, and his identification with a tusked boar suggest the possibility that the sacrificial boars represent those who confuse the kinship system. This possibility is strengthened by the father's claim that the nine younger brothers are his sons, while he refuses to have any dealings with To-wewe. This could signify that the eldest son is no longer his son, hence an outsider. The myth also seems to suggest that until there were kinship disputes based on the probability of incest, there was no need for the Maki rite. Finally, the myth speaks of two forms of incest: sibling (matrilineal) and mother-son (patrilineal). Could this reflect the two kinship modes (sibling/matrilineal and mother-child/patrilineal)? A look at another myth tends to confirm these ideas about kinship.

The Myth of the Creation of Pete-hul

THE ISLAND OF Vao (a smaller island off Malekula) contains several double-villages. Pete-hul is one of those villages. The mythological account of the creation of Pete-hul helps illuminate the importance of the transition from matrilineal to patrilineal descent. Ta-ghar, a mythical being, is considered the "creator of all men and things" (217). According to the myth, Ta-ghar caused a *memel* fruit to fall to the ground. The fall caused the fruit to split in two—one half becoming a man, one half becoming a woman. Following sexual intercourse four sons were born who became the founders of the four quarters of Pete-hul. One of the sons was Na-va-gharu-kalat. According to historical accounts and genealogies, Na-va-gharu-kalat was neither a deity, such as Ta-ghar, nor mythological, such as the man and woman who came from the *memel* fruit. Most likely he was from a culture with a patrilineal kinship system. Layard claims that Na-va-gharu-kalat arrived with his brothers on the island around 1680 (170). At that time the kinship system, which had been matrilineal, was thrown into confusion, and the wars over kinship and marriage began. Basing his assumptions on these accounts, Layard concludes that Na-va-gharu-kalat aggressively asserted himself on behalf of the patrilineal immigrants, "telling them to 'keep watch on the beach Kowu, and, if any stranger comes ashore, to kill him and bring him to me to cut up,' evidently for the whole community to eat" (167). This speech is credited with being the start of all subsequent fighting.

Perhaps this fighting is referred to in the previous story of To-wewe. If that is true, then perhaps Na-va-gharu-kalat is represented in the story as the father (the father of the village), and To-wewe represents a banished son of the woman who became Na-va-gharu-kalat's wife and mother of subsequent sons. This "stranger" landing on the beach has to be killed because he incestuously threatens the newly established patrilineal kinship system. The accounts of To-wewe and Na-va-gharu-kalat both tend to confirm Layard's belief that pig sacrifice replaced human sacrifice, which occurred as a result of kinship struggles. Among several significant customs introduced by the immigrant patrilineal culture were penis wrappers (men walked around nude in the matrilineal cultures) and penile incisions. Quite possibly these patrilineal traits reflect something of the hostility between the sexes, which is less prevalent in the matrilineal cultures.

Le-hev-hev: Guardian Ghost of the World of the Dead

IN THE MINDS of the participants of the Maki rite, the Guardian Ghost, Le-hev-hev, represents the ultimate and continual object to be overcome through the Maki. Le-hev-hev stands as the transitional barrier between the land of the living and that of the dead. It is affiliated with the spider who weaves a web to capture its prey. Erich Neumann argued that it is associated "with a giant bivalve that when opened resembles the female sexual organ, and in shutting endangers man and beast (1963, 177). It is a being men fear because it represents anti-being, the loss of self. "Le-hev-hev means: that which draws us to It so that It can devour us" (Layard 1942, 218). According to informants, Le-hev-hev is the reason why men perform their rites, why they dance and sacrifice pigs. In other words, from a conscious, ideological point of view, the Maki rite (the ritual cycle lasting fifteen to twenty years) is a "prophylactic against Le-hev-hev through the sacrifice of innumerable tusked boars" (256).

Layard believes that the function of the Maki rite is to protect the men moving through the graded society from the destructive anger of the ancestors symbolically embodied in and represented by the devouring Guardian Ghost Le-hev-hev. The ancestors most angry are those of the matrilineal line, which had suffered from the introduction of patrilineal descent. In the Maki rite the male representatives of the matrilineal line (the mother's brothers and mother's mother's brothers) demand special propitiation. The Maki then is both a kinship rite, which includes ritual payment to the matrilineal line as well as to Le-hev-hev, the mythical representative of the matrilineal ancestors. In the mythology of the death journey, this Guardian Ghost seeks to devour the dead man's soul before it can reach the land of the dead. After death each man must make his way through a difficult· labyrinth. Layard notes five main traits of the labyrinth, which he argues are universal: (1)it always has to do with death and rebirth (either life after death or ritual rebirth as a part of initiations); (2) it is usually connected with a cave; (3) the labyrinth is usually found at the entrance to the cave; (4) the being in charge of the labyrinth and the cave is invariably a woman; and (5) the labyrinth is overcome by a man (652).

As part of the ordeal through the labyrinth, the dead man offers a dead pig's soul instead of his own to the Guardian Ghost, and he is able to continue his journey to the land of the dead. Layard suggests that the Maki represents a dual purpose within the male natives' lives: to facilitate the urge to acquire higher and higher social ranking and to neutralize the fear of being devoured by the "primal force from which he has with so much exertion extricated himself and into which he is therefore in constant danger of falling back" (256). Layard claims that the Guardian Ghost "represents the reverse side of the social structure" (256). If the social structure is dominated by the immigrated patrilineal structure, then the reverse side would be the earlier matrilineal system, an earlier stratum of culture represented by the now terrifying Le-hev-hev.

But is Le-hev-hev simply a representation of the matrilineal side of society? Is it at all possible that Le-hev-hev might in fact be a powerful and sacred being believed in by the earlier matrilineal society? If that is the case, would it make sense to assume that her attributes had been a bit more positive at some time earlier in her history? I suggest that the introduction of the patrilineal, patriarchal sky god (Ta-ghar) was probably accompanied by the degradation of an earlier cult and mythology (assuming that it could not be eliminated without the elimination of the women it represented) (cf. Neumann 1963, 177). Layard claims that Le-hev-hev is the male native's "own and society's underside" (1942, 256). Neumann broadens this into a universal psychological state: "The whole of mankind and assuredly of primitive mankind . . . is involved in the struggle against the suction of the unconscious and its regressive lure; and this is the terrible aspect of the Feminine" (1963, 175). In this Jungian scheme Le-hev-hev is equated with the matrilineal ancestors, which are equated with the mothers, which are equated with the feminine, which is equated with the unconscious. I believe this Jungian theory does not contradict the theory I have been presenting. The male desire to climb ever higher and the fear of being devoured are certainly compatible with the two narcissistic structures—the grandiose self and (the dread of) the idealized mother imago. But the Jungian position fails to keep the importance of the social (kinship conflict and kinship stability) to the Maki rite at the center of the interpretation. Likewise, the myth cannot explain a ritual that gave rise to the myth. A Jungian interpretation confuses the origins of the dread of Le-hev-hev. The dread stems from self-object experiences, which are neither of the subject nor of the object, but are a transitional experience in the mind of the developing infant and affected by a second and independent experience in the mind of the mother, and later the father and culture. Because dread has no object, the dread becomes fear and the object becomes the mother. This will become clearer as we examine the symbolic elements in the ritual sacrifice of pigs.

RITUALS

THE FIFTEEN- TO twenty-year Maki rite is subdivided into two cycles of rites: Low Maki and High Maki. During many of the rites comprising both cycles, pigs are sacrificed. I have chosen to examine one such sacrifice—the culminating Great Sacrifice in the fourth year of Low Maki. A few days before the day on which the pigs are to be sacrificed, each Maki-man travels to all those who have promised him pigs. The donors consist of the Maki-man's sons-in-law and brothers-in-law. Maki-men are those who sacrifice pigs in order to move up the graded society. Their ultimate goal is to obtain a soul in order to live in the land of the dead. Conversely, women do not sacrifice because, according to men, they have no souls. This makes some sense from what we have seen in the review of myths. If a man is trying to escape the power of the matrilineal system and the women who represent it, and to claim power for himself through patriliny, then a woman with a soul on the other side of life would be the last person a man would want to meet.

Pigs are graded according to their body and tusk size. Two days before the sacrifice, all the lesser pigs are tied to stakes along the middle of an area called the dancing-ground. After a ritual dance proclaiming what is to take place, message yams (the same species of yams from the To-wewe story of incest and sacrifice) are carried to each village on Vao by witnesses to the examination of the pigs. Those who are invited from the villages arrive at the site of the forthcoming sacrifice and join in a dance that continues until midnight, after which everyone retires to rest up for the dancing and sacrificing to follow.

After a day of rest, the dance resumes the following evening and continues until dawn of the next (third) day. Following several lesser rites, a single pig is killed to mark the end of the all-night rites. Several hours later the participants, after another, briefer rest period, arrive again for the presentation of the pigs. Each Maki-man expects a tusked boar from his sons-in-law and his brothers-in-law. In an elaborate ceremony called the "circling rite," each graded pig is presented by the donor and his wife (either a daughter or a sister of the Maki-man). This procedure takes some time and afterwards the guests again retire. While they are away, the one hundred boars to be sacrificed are tied up to the one hundred stakes. The one hundred stakes are on the upper or men's side. To one hundred stakes on the lower or women's side are tied one hundred fowl (fowl, like women, are not graded). A reed screen around the animals, called a "birth enclosure," is erected.

Everyone now reassembles at the site. The introducing line shakes down the screen, exposing the animals and the dolmen (altar) upon which the highest-graded tuskers will be sacrificed by the chief Maki-men (those attaining the highest grade). The men of the introducing descent line gather at the center of the ritual ground and sing a chant about the Maki, representing it as "a canoe from afar that has now landed on the shore and has disgorged its cargo of men and tusked boars. This means, of course, that the day of sacrifice has at last arrived" (Layard 1942, 390). The Maki-men first kill the fowl and then the boars by hitting them on their heads with clubs. Those who are receiving a new low-rank title kill their chief tuskers at this time and assume their new ranks and social identity.

The chief Maki-men who are to receive the highest rank through the sacrifice of high-grade tuskers now try to approach the dolmen. At this time each chief Maki-man's mother's brothers symbolically keep him from approaching the dolmen to perform the sacrifice. In their capacity as guards, his mother's brothers represent, according to Layard, "the female line of descent represented by the figure of the Guardian Ghost" (395). And "the dolmen symbolizes at one and the same time the tomb, the cave of the dead . . . and the mother's womb out of which they are to be reborn" (395). In order to reach the dolmen the Maki-man makes a present of a lesser pig to his mother's brothers and the sacrifice then takes place. With the sacrifice the new title is assumed, and later the boar is eaten, "most probably by the mother's brothers" (393). The Maki-man retires and observes eating and sexual restrictions.

INTERPRETATION

I HAVE TRIED to include enough detail of social structure, mythology, and rites to now attempt an intelligible interpretation. Working from the rite back to the myths and social structure, I suspect that Layard is correct in his interpretation of both the dolmen and the mother's brothers. It would seem that there is a symbolic incest occurring, further reflected in the To-wewe story. And the reason for this incest quite possibly has to do with the change over from a matrilineal to a patrilineal kinship system. Thus, what cannot be tolerated in reality because of the violence it creates is enacted in a ritual. But why the sacrifice? Why not simply have a bacchanalia-like celebration? Because there is more to the sacrifice than the desire for incest.

The announcement of a canoe landing on the shore with its cargo of men and pigs and the immediate start of the sacrificing reenacts the orders of Na-va-gharu-kalat cited earlier. Certainly the sacrifice and eating of pigs reflect aspects of an earlier (and clandestinely continued) practice of ritualized cannibalism, if not human sacrifice. Layard reports not only that cannibalism occurred, but that it had "formed an integral part of the larger and more embracing rite of human sacrifice" (619). Although he notes the ritual importance of kinship and of ritual homicide and cannibalism, Layard offers no insight into the relationship between kinship and human sacrifice. That is probably because he associated human sacrifice with cannibalism rather than with kinship conflicts or war.

As I noted earlier, one of the apparent functions of the Maki rite is somehow to put a stop to kinship-induced wars and to restore peace. The natives admit as much. If that is the case, how does the sacrifice of pigs (or even of humans) accomplish this? We can see in the To-wewe story that To-wewe wants to put an end to the fighting. But his violation of kinship rules is also the cause of fighting. His self-sacrifice and apparent identification with the pig suggests that the pig represents the man guilty of confusing the kinship. That is to say, the Maki-man who pours his blood (symbolized by the pig's blood) into his mother's womb (symbolized by the dolmen) has to die. His rebirth through the graded Maki society increases his distance from the power within the matriliny (i.e., the mothers).

The fact that it is the mother's brothers who have to be placated seems to suggest this possibility. The kinship conflicts appear to answer a great many puzzles. The matrilineal-patrilineal conflict also seems apparent in the imbalance between pigs and fowl as well as by the fact that the men who control the ritual life of the society do not believe that women have souls. Perhaps the rite is not so much about either kinship systems (both of which are male controlled) as it is over tension between the sexes. Layard noted this connection between warfare and tension between the sexes. He states that wars are "fought almost entirely on questions involving the prestige of one group over against another, in order to maintain the existing order of society by wreaking vengeance on any who seek to disturb it. Now the order of society is based on kinship, and kinship is based on regulations concerning the relations between the sexes. It is not surprising that the immediate cause of almost all wars is a sexual one, such as adultery or elopement" (588).

If a function of the Maki is to maintain the social structure while avoiding war, then one obvious yet significantly overlooked purpose is the elimination of conflicts between the sexes, which lead to war. If sacrifice is about power, if sacrifice is about a surrogate victim killed to maintain order, and if the violence of the act is somehow essential for sacrificial efficacy, then the sacrifice of pigs could represent the killing of those who could have or did at one time have intercourse with the women of the village, that is, matrilineal insiders who were now considered outsiders—the ones landing on the beach, the ones that had to be killed. The question remains, however, how a pig's death satisfies this possibility. I suggest that the substitution of a pig for a man occurs on two ideological levels: that of the man as the cause of the kinship wars, and that of the man who substitutes one soul for his own as he acquires a new social identity.

The fact that the pig is related in some way to Le-hev-hev as well, however, suggests that there are other factors operating in the ritual. Perhaps Neumann is correct in suggesting that the Guardian Ghost represents the dread of the feminine. But I doubt whether the dread is something as archetypal as the dread of the unconscious. The dread is more concrete than that. It is possible that the sacrifice could symbolize a deeper subliminal message to the women of the village that they are nothing, that they have no souls, that their procreative power is acquired, superseded, and controlled by the gradual acquisition of a soul by the men through a symbolic death and rebirth controlled entirely by men. And, if women try to leave with the "men in the canoe" (i.e., break the reproductive rules), violence will be done to them and their suitors. Thus, the reason for the message in the first place has to do with both the male need for prestige and their fear of women.

I think the social situation could very well support this argument. "A woman taken in adultery," writes Layard, "runs the risk of being killed on the spot, if her husband is so minded, and no one would blame him" (199). Or "A small pebble of lava would be made red hot, and used to brand the unhappy woman's body, nine times out of ten this would result in death" (199). Other punishments cited for a woman running away include that of hamstringing her, or suspending her over a fire and roasting her knees and feet. Other lesser treatments included beating and stoning. Adulterous men, in sharp contrast, had the option of paying a fine.

These reports by Layard are repeated throughout other areas of Melanesia. As Counts notes, "many Pacific societies consider a certain level of family violence to be normal and acceptable" (1990, 3). In an account of male antagonism toward women in the New Guinea Highlands, violence toward women includes rape and gang rape and "an angry man may focus his attack on a woman by cutting, burning, or otherwise mutilating her genital and reproductive organs" (Gelber 1986, 25). These incidents are not the isolated acts of psychotics but rather reflect a cultural pattern that Layard had recognized some sixty years earlier on Malekula..

My suspicion is that the fear of loss of control of women and enacting the message not to leave are both evident in the Maki rite itself. In Low Maki, for example, at one point the Maki-men dance around waving branches and singing a women's song connected with the killing of the home-bred circle tusker. It is a song performed by the women on the day of the chief sacrifices of High Maki. In High maki the wives of the Maki-men perform this dance and song with their husbands. According to Layard:

> When the dance is over, the wives of the Maki-men, now stationed at one end of the dancing-ground, drop their bamboos

and run across the dancing-ground, and are pursued by one, sometimes two, Maki-men waving leafy branches. . . . Those on the middle of the dancing-ground fall back on either side to make way for *the fleeing women, who run down to the shore*. The waving of the branches is called "beating the women," though in fact no beating occurs, and possibly represents a cleansing of the dancing-ground from the contact of women. (1942, 424)

Immediately after this the main sacrificial act begins. Layard's "possible" interpretation of these beatings representing a cleansing seems a bit naive. The juxtaposition of the beating, fleeing to the shore (where the canoe is to land announcing the start of the sacrifice), and the sacrificing seems to me to add a dimension to the nature and function of sacrifice. Given this evidence, it is no wonder that Layard was unable to spend any private time with the women to obtain their own accounts.

Having thus suggested that the pig sacrifices of Malekula express or represent something of the male psychic apparatus, I want to present a Kohutian explanation of that apparatus. The issues of gender conflict, kinship struggles, and wars are based, according to Layard, almost entirely on questions of male prestige and the wreaking of vengeance on any who seek to disturb that prestige (embodied in the social order). Prestige is also evident in the male native's desire to climb ever higher through the graded system. On the other hand, there we also note a strong element of fear or anxiety—the fear of being devoured by what Layard calls "the primeval force from which he has with so much exertion extricated himself and into which he is therefore in constant danger of falling back" (256). Prestige and fear function as part of what Turner would call an experiential process represented by a continuum of meaning expressed in the symbolic rituals. The fear of annihilation by something powerful and the desire to attain one's own power, then, are the two primary psychological elements in the male use of ritual sacrifice on Malekula. The first point I want to make then, is that both prestige and the fear of an idealized, symbolic "primeval force" are part of a related experiential psychological process. Because it is experiential, we need a psychological explanation that can account for this idea of an experiential continuum.

Kohut's two self-objects (the grandiose self and the idealized parent imago) together provide such an explanatory apparatus. Prestige, along with the related self-esteem, grandiosity, exhibitionism, and so on, become activated during the narcissistic period of development. Their first pre-structure is the grandiose self. Idealizations of omnipotent self-objects—experienced either as beneficent or malignant—originate in the same narcissistic period as the prestructural idealized parent imago. Initially the idealized parent imago is experienced by the grandiose self as part of itself. Metapsychologically, they are both self-objects—pre-structural, pre-symbolic, and therefore presexual and preoedipal. Under even the most healthy developments, these two self-objects can remain split-off parts of the structured self. The more split-off, the more terrifying can be the experience of their intrusion into the self.

I suggest that the Guardian Ghost Le-hev-hev is a culturally externalized and accepted symbolic representation of a negatively experienced idealized parent imago. Le-hev-hev's identity as somehow female and yet not quite female suggests this presexual period. Yet also symbolized by the spilling of the Maki-man's surrogate blood on the dolmen (itself a symbol of both the womb and the tomb) is the desire for merger with Le-hev-hev. The idealized self-object may be feared for its fragmenting effect on the self, but there is an ambivalence toward such a merger. In Kohut's terms, the spilling of incestuous blood on the dolmen represents a telescoping of narcissistic desire or hunger for the idealized self-object onto later oedipal themes. Thus, the ritual sacrifice expresses a longed-for merger with an idealized self-object. At the same time the potential for narcissistic merger creates a sense of anxiety or fear. Psychoanalytically, the self fears its own dedifferentiating fragmentation. Because the anxiety is the dread of that which is desired most, it contains a high degree of ambivalence. I am here arguing that this anxiety stems from a pre-structural narcissistic stage of development. The cultural relativity of the social structures that foster what is to be feared may indicate that their content is not the cause of the anxiety. In other words, this anxiety is a response to *pre-structural* elements, which create and fuel the particular cultural objects of fear.

This leads me to state further that the pig sacrifices express a hunger for *and* a denial of narcissistic merger. The intrusion into the self by hunger for merger is powerfully enthralling. Such intrusion flows from parts of the grandiose self and idealized self-object not integrated into a cohesive self. These narcissistic split-off parts can be projected onto and identified with actual and/or imagined marginal beings (in our example, Le-hev-hev and pigs), but these, in turn, are symbols of other beings—notably women (Le-hev-hev) and men who could also control the women (embodied in the pigs). In the end, the sacrifice denies the very merger it seeks to enact because the longed-for merger with, and dread of, the idealized self-object by the grandiose self stems from a prestructural, pre-symbolic narcissism, and no symbol or symbolic structure such as a sacrifice can ultimately contain or express the merger.

A FINAL CONSIDERATION

JOHN LAYARD WAS one of the first generation of anthropologists sensitized to the discoveries made by Freud and Jung in the early years of the psychoanalytic movement. Although Freud and Jung have been dismissed by most anthropologists as inadequate and ethnographically sloppy, the same cannot be said of Layard. While his psychological interpretations may be suspect, his ethnographic descriptions of Malekulan society remain respected (Allen 1981). As a matter of fact, the work of anthropologists sensitized to feminist critiques of gender and culture describe conditions on other Melanesian cultures remarkably similar to those described by Layard. Roger Kessing's descriptions of Kwaio society (1982, 1987), Ann Chowning's work on Kove culture (1987), and Michael Young's accounts of Kalauna life (1987) show that much of Layard's observations were accurate. The antagonism between and segregation of the sexes, the sexual causes of war and ritual, and the use of ritual by men to acquire prestige and power, all are seen over and over again in many Melanesian societies. Gilbert Herdt (1981a, 1981b, 1982) has ventured a significant psychological interpretation of male rituals in Papua, New Guinea, which likewise acts as further affirmation of Layard's work on Malekula. The list goes on. The point I am making is not that these studies of New Guinea Highland societies can be compared to Layard's study of Malekula, but that there are issues common to both settings and every reason to believe that Layard's ethnography was consistent with the modern studies.

FOURTEEN

The Episcopal Eucharist: Women, Sin, and Christ

ANTHROPOLOGY BEGAN AS the Western intellectual study of exotic and "primitive" non-Western cultures. The histories of these cultures were not readily accessible to anthropologists because the indigenous populations had no written language and hence no written history. The oral histories that existed were often contained within mythologies, which further complicated their objectivity. Over the course of its history, anthropology has out of necessity and, I think, reluctantly given up its desire to study the "savage mind" or the culture unadulterated by Western influences. Because of the West's near-universal influence on every culture, anthropology has had to become more historically oriented in its approach to non-Western cultures. Contemporary anthropologists now study the culture *and* history of a people (*see* Comaroff 1985).

With the decline in the number of unstudied cultures (as well as the grants to pay for the studies), the increase in the number of anthropology graduate students, and the rise of non-Western indigenous anthropologists, anthropology has begun to apply its mode of observation and interpretation to Western culture. Anthropology's reluctance to study the West is, of course, due in part to the fact that the academic disciplines of history and sociology had already laid claim to the West. In a parallel process, the history of religions was reluctant to study Western religions because history and theology had laid claim to that. I suspect that another reason anthropology and the history of religions have not studied Western religion has as much to do with the fact that both anthropologists and historians of religion belong to the traditions that they would be studying. One's own

163

narcissism might be activated were the God of Abraham, Isaac, and Jacob or God the Father of Jesus Christ or Jesus Christ the Son of God referred to as "non-empirical entities" (something anthropologists would find easier to do in the study of non-Western religions).

The anthropological study of Western religious rituals, then, is a very recent development; I hope to show in this chapter that its time has come. Although I have chosen to study the eucharist as it is practiced in the Episcopal church, USA, I contend that the conclusions I draw from this study of the Episcopal ritual have application for the study of American religions in general. In this brief study I do not intend to review the liturgical or theological history of the eucharist. There are many such histories available (*see* Cullman 1953). As a way of examining the ritual, I want to present an anthropological context for a psychoanalytic understanding of the eucharist somewhat similar to the Malekulan example. I have again divided this chapter into social context, mythology, and ritual. I hope Kohut's concepts are familiar enough to the reader to allow me to use them more freely in the analysis, thus avoiding the need for a separate section on the psychological interpretation.

THE SOCIAL CONTEXT OF THEOLOGY

IN HIS SOCIOLOGICAL study of four Chicago churches in the 1960s, Michael Ducey (1977) argued for a distinction between what he terms "mass rituals" and "interaction rituals." In a mass ritual an audience collectively reacts to the performance by religious specialists of a cluster of sacred symbols, actions, words, and even music. It is this unified response that characterizes the ritual as a *mass* ritual. In an interaction ritual, the audience participates in a response to the cluster of religious symbols and actions. They may also interact with each other. It is the multifocal interaction that determines the character of an *interaction* ritual. According to these definitions, the Episcopal eucharist is a mass ritual. Mass ritual is characteristic of mainline denominations. Mainline denominations are comprised of members who maintain the current social status quo. Their liturgies will not vary to any great degree from parish to parish. As a matter of fact, the unchanging nature of the liturgy is a further sign of the often unspoken desire to have things stay the way they are, the logic being that the older or more original is more valuable. Even the liturgical movement of the last hundred years within the Episcopal church succeeded more in restoring the ancient ways rather than establishing any new forms of worship.

Victor and Edith Turner have argued that neither penance nor the eucharist are rites of passage. Both "sacraments in one aspect form an admirable system of social control" (1978, 32). This control has been a feature recognized by psychoanalysts as well. According to Erich Fromm, the Church's manipulation of the population's feelings of anger toward authority is part of its history. The Church was able to deflect the anger against God and earthly authorities in a reproach of the self by increasing the sense of guilt to an almost unbearable level, thereby deflecting the anger away from those with power onto those without power—the suffering mass. At the same time "it offered itself to these suffering masses as a good and loving father, since the priests granted pardon and expiation for the guilt feelings which they themselves had engendered" (Fromm 1955, 66). Thus the Church becomes the Great Mother and her male heirs (the fathers) control the only way to atone for sin and receive grace through the self-annihilation of the Son. While the worship developed by such a system has remained remarkably constant, the social conditions within the American Christian churches have changed a great deal, giving rise to fierce social and theological debates..

I have chosen to review the social contexts of four theological issues of the second half of the twentieth century within some American Christian churches—the Episcopal church in particular. These theological occasions are evidence for the continued *psychotheological* relationship between the eucharist as the central liturgical rite of the Episcopal church and women as the origin of sin and defilement. The term *psychotheological view* is from Bakan. The position I develop differs from Bakan's Freudian model of the eucharist as a symbolic reenactment of an infanticidal wish by the fathers to kill their sons. Infanticidal wishes on the part of the fathers are secondary to and fueled by narcissistic wishes of the fathers toward the mothers of the sons (Bakan 1966, 197–236). Such psychotheological evidence is no less apparent now than it was during the time of Tertullian or Paul or Moses or any of the "fathers" of the Western religious tradition. The four theological issues I will review are: (1) the ordination of women; (2) the sexuality of clergy (i.e, celibacy in Roman Catholicism, homosexuality in all churches); (3) creationism; and (4) abortion. All four issues, while in the forefront of Episcopal theological debates, form a significant context for appreciating the legitimating power of the unconscious, male eucharistic ideology. All four also indicate the male need for power and prestige.

Apostolic Succession, Ordination, and Women

NANCY JAY HAS argued that male priesthood and the apostolic succession was established as a means of maintaining a male patrilineal descent, which controls the central sacrificial act of the Church in the eucharist. Three related factors came together to form the liturgical center of the Church: "the Eucharist as 'blood sacrifice,' the Christian clergy as a specific sacrificing priesthood, and the unilineal organization of the priesthood as exclusive inheritors of apostolic authority" (Jay 1985, 300). Jay points out that such an ecclesiastical development finds no validation either in the New Testament or in the history of the early Church. She concludes that understanding the sociology of the eucharist depends on the "recognition of the power of sacrifice as a ritual instrument for establishing and maintaining an enduring male-dominated social order" (304). Such a social order is evident in the Episcopal church, where clerical hierarchy is based on apostolic succession—the bishop and priests being the only persons who can celebrate the eucharist.

The women's ordination movement and the concurrent liturgical movement have not eliminated the central place of Christ's sacrifice within the eucharist, although Eucharistic Prayers B and C (*Book of Common Prayer* 1977) do not emphasize the crucifixion as sacrifice to the extent that Prayer A does. However, just as in the Roman Catholic church, the theology of the eucharist remains debatable, and the resolution of the conflict that gives bishops authority to ordain women as priests is still not accepted by a large number of church members, both laity and clergy. One group in particular, the Episcopal Synod of America (ESA) absolutely rejects the ordination and seeks its own non-geographical province (the so-called 10th Province) because of it.

In 1974 at an Episcopal church in Philadelphia, several women deacons were ordained priests by bishops of the Episcopal church. The ordination came as no surprise to most in the Episcopal church. The House of Bishops had voted previously to remove all obstacles to women's ordination, only to have the resolution voted down by laity and priests at a general convention. Following what quickly came to be recognized as an "unauthorized" ordination, the members of the Episcopal church were forced to reckon with women's ordination as a fait accompli. At a later general convention, members voted and approved in principle that women could be called to the priesthood as certainly as men could be called. Ecclesiastically the issue appeared resolved. Some members (laity and clergy) threatened to leave the Episcopal church; some did. But, for the most part, any decisions about women's ordination moved underground and out of sight, or so it seemed. Antagonism toward women as priests surfaced again in 1989 when an African-American woman was elected and then consecrated bishop.

The ordination of women as priests gave the members of the church a new model of ministry, an alternative view of what a woman could be. It created a different idea of gender role. In spite of this, women Episcopal priests remain underemployed, earn less money than their male counterparts, and are more likely to be found in the smaller, less-appealing parishes. Men priests still get the better jobs (McGuire 1981, 95; *see also* Ruether and Keller 1981; Verdesi 1976). Arguably the same analysis could be made about women in all those traditionally male roles that have been opened to women. My position, however, is that the male function of sacrifice psychologically precludes a woman from performing the act. Thus, at the deepest levels of the male and male-identified psyche (which may also include those of women priests) is the fear and resentment of the power of women. A woman performing a ritual sacrifice can evoke deep resentment. For those who harbor no such resentment, the idea of the eucharist as sacrifice has probably lost its psychological connection to women and sin. Of course if the meaning of the eucharist changes too much, and with it the sacrifice of Christ for the sins of humanity, then a woman at the Lord's Table may cease to be such a thorn in so many sides. I doubt that can happen without abandoning a theology in which a child of God is sacrificed for the sins of humanity. As long as the Church's image of God remains primarily male, Christ's death is seen as a sacrifice of a son, and the eucharist remains the central liturgical act of the Episcopal church, women as celebrating priests will remain psychologically problematic.

Human Sexuality and the Church

THE WOMEN'S AND gay movements of the last thirty years have brought the question of the meaning of sex and its place in the Church to the forefront. I have included the issues of celibacy within the Roman Catholic church and homosexuality within both the Roman and Anglican churches in the same discussion because they are psychologically related to the same underlying fear of women and the need to control their power. The history of male celibacy within the priesthood is related to the issue of women and sin. Jay contends that one original function of the celibate priest was to maintain an apostolic lineage of "fathers" without any dependence on women for its origins or maintenance (1985, 301–3). In other words, celibacy along with priesthood provides the power of "fatherhood" without the help of mothers or the necessity of becoming actual fathers. Historically, another problem with non-celibate priests is that those who had children disrupted the lines of inheritance. The renewed call by both Catholic priests and laity for priests to be allowed to marry is a direct assault on the original psychosocial reason for the priesthood in the first place. Psychologically, it would place men within the context of the very power from which the priesthood had sought to extricate itself with the eucharistic sacrifice.

The debate over homosexuality follows a different path of unconscious rationalization but ends up with the same result. Homosexuality within the priesthood sends a message to women that should not be sent. It is not the male homosexual priest that is the only issue here. He may be simply following out the logic of the sacrificing priesthood's relation to women and sin. This is not the place to replay the unconscious identification and anxiety heterosexuals may feel towards homosexuals, but such identification cannot be ignored either. For the purposes of this book, however, it is the female counterpart that is the real threat to the male narcissistic need for power over women. The fact that lesbians reject men where men's narcissism is vulnerable fuels an additional fear of homosexuality in the priesthood. Gay priests may be despised because psychologically they do not want to control, or be controlled by, women. Lesbians, on the other hand, are hated and feared because they do not need men. Several unofficial groups within the Episcopal church—Episcopalians United, the Episcopal Synod of America, and the Prayer Book Society—continue to resist the ordination of homosexuals and the use of inclusive language in liturgical texts. I have already mentioned the ESA's desire to form the 10th Province.

Creationism and Women

THE CREATIONISM DEBATE is evident among the more fundamentalist groups, yet even the Episcopal church has creationist advocates.

As in the above two issues, there is a psychological process here that parallels the theological one. The well-known theological debate between scientific theory and biblical revelation hides a deeper psychological need reflecting male and male-identified narcissism. When the creationist says that God created the world in the way that is reported in Genesis, that person is in effect saying that sex has nothing to do with how God (or Nature) works. The male God of the Genesis story creates without sex. There is no need for a female presence in the creation of the world. Indeed woman came out of man, a reversal of biological fact. Couple that with the belief that women are the origin of defilement and sin, and the belief that the same male God and his son have saved the world from sins which go back to women, and the narcissistic dimension of creationism may seem a bit clearer. I wonder if remarks by former Secretary of the Interior James Watt—that because of the Second Coming we need not be overly concerned about the environment—could be interpreted as a further diminution of the value of *Mother* Earth and women.

Abortion and the Church

THOSE WHO MAINTAIN that the conception of human life is sacred and should take precedence over the decisions of a woman about her body have many thousands of years of history to back up their claim that society can decide what a woman must do with her body. It is echoed in the marriage service of the Episcopal *Book of Common Prayer*, in which the priest may ask, "Who gives this bride to be married?" The ideology of women as possessions is ancient indeed. To allow women not only the power to give birth, but to allow them the *choice* as to whether that should happen—that is a wound to male narcissism that for some cannot be endured. Within the Episcopal church there is a small but vocal group of clergy and laity who are strongly against abortion. It would be interesting to see where this group stands in relation to the previous three psychotheological issues.

Contextual Conclusion

MY PURPOSE IN presenting these four issues is to try and achieve some sense of old and significant sentiments that have psychological dimensions, but which are usually debated ideologically. Their presence does not "prove" the theory I have been developing, but I hope they at least enflesh it. A male and male-identified psychology fueling such attitudes and reactions toward women may be more obvious in the social life of Malekula than within the social context of the Episcopal church. But the reality of that psychology is, I believe, nevertheless apparent in the social context and veiled in the liturgical context of the eucharist.

The term *eucharist* as the Lord's Supper or Thanksgiving of the Lord's Supper is not actually used in the New Testament. In order to understand the eucharist as sacrifice, I have to back up a bit and first understand Christ's death as sacrifice. In the ritual practiced by the Episcopal church, the eucharist enacts and recalls both the Last Supper and the death of Christ on the cross. These two events comprise the dual function of the eucharist as both a communal meal and expiatory sacrifice. In the remainder of this chapter, I focus on the relation of the death of Christ to sacrifice, women, and the eucharist.

THE MYTHOLOGY OF CHRIST AND SIN

MOST CHRISTAIN GROUPS believe that God became human (a male human) and offered himself to take away the sins of the world. The Gospel of John expresses this position in two verses: "And the Word (of God) became flesh and dwelt among us. . . . 'Behold, the Lamb of God who takes away the sins of the world'" (John 1:24, 29). The Nicene Creed (325 A.D.) states that Christians "believe in one Lord Jesus Christ . . . who was made flesh for our salvation." From a psychoanalytic point of view, within this myth sin is a transgression of boundaries, which necessitates a sacrifice to restore sacred order (in theological terms, salvation from sin, evil, and death). In exploring the symbolism of evil, Paul Ricoeur notes a phenomenological relation between sin, fault, and defilement. Symbols of evil point back to a terror of defilement, a position nearly identical to that of Mary Douglas. "Dread of the impure and rites of purification [here Ricoeur has in mind the Near Eastern rituals exemplified in the Old Testament] are in the background of all our feelings and all our behavior relating to fault" (1967, 25). Ricoeur defines defilement as "an act that evolves an evil, an impurity, a fluid, a mysterious and harmful something that acts dynamically—that is to say magically" (25).

The problem for Ricoeur is the move from the symbol of evil to an earlier dreadful experience of defilement. In the economy of defilement, Ricoeur is "struck by the importance and the gravity attached to the violation of interdictions of a sexual character" (128). But in addition to sexual defilement, Ricoeur adds the terror of defilement through ethically neutral activities; he gives as examples "the frog that leaps into the fire, the hyena that leaves its excrements in the neighborhood of a tent" (27). And he notes the almost complete lack of defilement with such ethically evil acts as theft and lying, although homicide, the shedding of blood, risks some defilement in the same way as sexual phenomena, such as menstruation. Finally, Ricoeur notes the clear relation between defilement and illness, pain, and suffering. Theologically, the origin of illness, pain, suffering, as well as sin can be traced back to two related events: the fall of Adam at the hands of the woman Eve and the origin of each human life at the moment of conception in the womb of a woman. For the source of original sin as woman and the snake (nature?), see Gen. 3:12–16; for the source of sin within each individual, see Ps. 51:5: "in sin did my mother conceive me." May and Metzger contend that this is "a confession of the psalmist that his nature has been sinful even from the moment of conception" (1965, 694).

When Christ, the sacrificial Lamb of God, takes away the sins of the world, that sin has its origins in two qualities of defilement: one that "infects," and the other "a dread that anticipates the unleashing of the avenging wrath of the interdiction. These are the two traits that we no longer comprehend except as moments in the representation of evil that we have gone beyond" (Ricoeur 1967, 33). It is not necessary to search out the biblical examples that indicate that Ricoeur has done his phenomenological homework, even if the psychology of the bipolar characteristics of defilement escapes his interest. The psychological *effect* of sin, however, Ricoeur generalized to a "feeling of being abandoned" (48). It is no accident that the word "abandon" (from the French *abandon*) is the opposite of bind, bond, bound, and boundary (from the French *bander*, to bind up), which is also the meaning of the word *covenant*. In sin the connecting boundary (covenant) between a person or group and its core of social meaning (God) is broken. In order to restore the bond, the sin causing the abandonment is expiated through the sacrifice of an innocent victim. That victim is a god-man having the power to take on the sin and eliminate it through his death. Christ is the boundary or marginal being who stands between a God who calls a people back to covenant, and a people who experience sin, guilt, and abandon-

ment (without, according to Ricoeur's theory, being able to recall
the origins of all three in the pre-ethical experience of defilement).

Although the Genesis story places Woman at the core of sin
and defilement, most male commentators fail to explain the origin
of the myth of the Fall. Theodore Robinson, for example, believes a
woman's role in the Fall reflects women's position in Eastern society:
"The details of the woman's punishment are not certain, but it is
clear that we have here also the explanation of familiar facts, which
includes the social inferiority of women as it appears in the East"
(1920, 223). Adam and the biblical author(s) blame the socially in-
ferior woman for the Fall. This is a point against which only feminist
writers have argued with any obvious intentionality (*see* Daly 1973,
43–68). The message that Eve and Woman are the origin of sin and
death and still feared by men was conveyed in Tertullian's (c. 160–
240 A.D.) claim that women "are the devil's gateway. . . . How
easily you [women] destroyed man, the image of God. Because of
the death which you brought upon us, even the Son of God had to
die" (44). The execution of Jesus of Nazareth was rationalized into
a myth in which women were to blame.

In Ricoeur's analysis of sin, guilt, and abandonment, his concepts of dread and defilement recall Kohut's concept of narcissistic
anxiety. "Dread of the impure," writes Ricoeur, "is like fear, but already it faces a threat which, beyond the threat of suffering and death,
aims at the diminution of existence, a loss of the personal core" (1967,
41). This fear exists in the half-physical, half-ethical ambiguous world
of archaic self-objects. "Actions become evil" (move onto the ethical
plane of sin), continues Ricoeur, "in connection with the confession
of divine holiness, respect for interhuman ties, and self-esteem" (27).
Understood self-psychologically, actions become dreadful and thus
sinful only in relation to narcissism: the idealized parent imago ("divine holiness"), the grandiose self ("self-esteem"), and the narcissistic
transformation to empathy ("respect for interhuman ties"). In sin the
self is deflated via the infection (grandiose intrusions) and the interdiction of the avenging God (intrusions of the idealized parent imago). The sacrifice restores the tension gradient between the two self-
objects, leading to increased self-esteem and a view of God as more
empathic. Yet, it is important always to remember that these are finally male self-objects about which I am speaking.

After the sacrifice, Christ was raised from the dead, thereby
overcoming death itself, and he promised he will come again and

usher in the perfect kingdom of God. The eucharist became the central rite of the early Christian church in part because of the continuing delay of that Second Coming. The original sacrifice was combined with the Last Supper to be memorialized in the eucharist in which the celebrant proclaims: "Christ our passover is sacrificed for us." To which the people reply: "Therefore let us keep the feast" (1 Cor. 5:7–8).

THE RITUAL EUCHARIST: RITE TWO

THERE ARE SEVERAL authorized versions of the eucharist in the Episcopal church, which the bishop or priest can celebrate. These versions grew out of an ongoing liturgical movement, which culminated in the authorization by the Episcopal General Convention of 1976 of two primary rites of the Holy Eucharist. Rite One is in the traditional English found in the *Prayer Book* of 1928; Rite Two is in modern English. Yet both rites follow the same basic outline. I have chosen to analyze Rite Two. (For the sake of clarity, I will use initial uppercase letters when referring to words specifically capitalized in the *Book of Common Prayer*; otherwise I will use lowercase letters. Unless otherwise noted, all quotations from the Holy Eucharist are from Rite Two [*Book of Common Prayer* 1977, 355–66].) The rite is very similar to those followed by the Roman and Lutheran churches.

The Word of God

THE SERVICE OF the Holy Eucharist is divided into two main parts: the service of the Word and the service of Holy Communion. The service of the Word begins with a responsive acclamation, which affirms the Christian belief that God is the Father, that Christ is the son of God, as well as the belief in the Holy Spirit. It is in the name of this God that the participants were once baptized. Baptism into the faith is the only formal prerequisite for receiving communion.

According to Christian belief, the reason God became man was in order to take away the sins of the world. During Lent and other penitential times, an alternate acclamation may be used: "Blessed the Lord who forgives all our sins." To which the people reply: "His mercy endures for ever." The service could also begin with a Penitential Order in which would be said the Ten Commandments and a Confession of Sins. The Confession can also occur later in the ser-

vice. The logic of the Confession coming at the beginning of the
service of the Word stems from the belief that Christ came to take
away the sins of the world. Therefore, before the congregation can
hear and proclaim the word made flesh, it first acknowledges that it
is in a state of sin. The logic of the Confession following the Word
of God and preceding the Communion lies in the belief that without
knowledge of the Word of God, the congregation lacks the knowledge that it is in sin. Psychologically, the confession of sin embodies
the narcissistic experience of intrusive defilement of and abandonment by the maternal self-object.

Regardless of where the Confession occurs, it is followed by
the absolution declared by the celebrant. If the Confession occurs
after the Prayers of the People, the celebrant would proceed with the
Collect of Purity. This Collect takes much of its terminology from
the Psalms, particularly Psalm 51. In the Collect of Purity a significant self-object function of God is apparent. God is much like an
idealized parent imago—omnipotent and omniscient. According to
the Collect, everything that goes on within the inner life of the be-
lieving sinner is known to God. That inner life is filled with thoughts
that have to be cleansed—sinful thoughts, guilty thoughts, defiled
or stained thoughts. In the Psalm used in the Collect, the origin of
the sin needing to be cleansed has existed since the moment of conception: "Behold, I was brought forth in iniquity and in sin did my
mother conceive me" (Ps. 51:5). In this short Collect is veiled the
immense difference between Almighty God the Father and the mother's womb. Between the two stands the sinner, at a deep self-psychological level, asking the Father to cleanse him of his mother "by
the inspiration of your Holy Spirit." This redundancy seems to suggest that the Holy Spirit of the Father can create a heart cleansed of
the original, maternal stain.

Having praised the Trinity of God, the celebrant proceeds to a
Collect of the Day. The liturgical function of the Collect is to ask
God to grant the gifts God has promised. The psychological function
is to evoke the omnipotent, paternal self-object. The congregation is
now ready to hear the Word of God, which is hidden in scripture
(an Old Testament lesson, a psalm, an epistle, and a gospel reading).
These readings are followed by a sermon in which the celebrant usually preaches on the message and meaning of the lessons and gospel.
Following the sermon, the celebrant and congregation say together
the Nicene Creed. The Creed reflects the creative fatherhood of God.

The nature of Jesus Christ is confessed. The first part about Christ clearly indicates the unity of God the Father and Christ the Son. Both the Gospel and the Creed proclaim the eternal quality of Christ (the Word): the fact that the Word came from God, was created by God ("God from God"), and also *was* God at the same time (cf., "I and the Father are One" [John 10:30]). Both want to be clear that Christ is the Word of God that has always been. This is important in order to understand the meaning of the incarnation, particularly its relation to the virgin woman Mary. The Creed makes it clear that the birth through a woman is of the *eternal* Word of God, which has existed from the beginning with God and is not dependent on the woman for its existence. Here the Johannine theology reflects the reduction in the theological importance of the Mother. The Creed goes on to recount that Christ was killed "for our sake," that is, for our sins. It concludes with some general beliefs about the Holy Spirit, the Church, baptism, resurrection, and the kingdom of God still to come. The psychological function of belief in Christ is to overcome the experience of the sinful influence of the maternal self-object, both as abandoner and intrusive defiler.

Having heard the Word, the congregation proceeds to ask God for what it needs (i.e., for peace, its ministers and leaders, the earth; help for the old, the sick, the oppressed, the imprisoned; deliverance from danger and suffering; for hope). Each of these prayers is a specific form of asking for deliverance from the state of sin. For that reason, a general Confession of Sins follows the prayers (if one has not been said earlier). I have already suggested the hidden ideology and psychology of sin, so I will not go over the Confession. The celebrant then offers God's promise of absolution of sins to all who repent. After the absolution, all greet each other with the Peace of God. The Word of God has been proclaimed, the people have confessed both their faith and their sins (in whichever order), and now prepare to join one another at the Lord's table/altar for the Communion.

The Holy Communion

THE CELEBRANT MOVES to the table, signalling the liturgical move from the Word to the Sacrament of Holy Communion. There are four main activities in the Communion: the Offertory, the Great Thanksgiving, the Fraction, and the distribution of Holy Communion.

1. The Offertory. Here the bread and wine, as well as other expressions of the congregation's life and labor, are presented to God. But the main offering is the bread and wine which symbolize the body and blood of Christ, the sacrificial victim.

2. The Great Thanksgiving. I am using Eucharistic Prayer A, whose structure echoes that of the creeds and has its roots in the earliest documented Christian liturgies. It emphasizes the crucifixion as sacrifice. Prayer B emphasizes the incarnation. Prayer C emphasizes the creation and salvation in the Old Testament. Prayer D pulls together many of the themes from A, B, and C. The Thanksgiving asserts that Jesus Christ was sent to reconcile sinning people to God. Christ has accomplished this reconciliation through his self-sacrifice "in obedience to [God's] will." This is followed by the recounting of the Last Supper in which Christ invites the disciples to eat the bread, which is his body, and drink the wine, which is his blood, given and shed "for the forgiveness of sins." The celebrant and congregation then proclaim together the "mystery of faith": "Christ has died. / Christ has risen. / Christ will come again." The celebrant then proclaims that this sacrifice being celebrated is a memorial of human redemption and that the bread and wine are "by your Holy Spirit . . . the Body and Blood of your Son."

The consecration of the bread and wine symbolizes more than the bread and wine becoming the body and blood of Christ. The consecration also symbolizes Christ's body and blood becoming food and drink. The eating and drinking of the flesh and blood enables the consumer to incorporate and be incorporated by the nurturing body of Christ. The process parallels that of the nurturing body of the mother, which, I argue, is replaced by the body of Christ. In her study of a twelfth-century Cistercian community, Carolyn Bynum discovered that the image of Jesus as mother was an important devotional theme, based on biblical imagery. Bynum points out, however, that the images do not tell us much about what religious men thought of women or mothers. Rather "the monastic idea of mother-Jesus tells us . . . only what monks thought about Jesus and themselves" (1982, 167). Bynum notes that during the Middle Ages, "in the cult of the Sacred Heart, they frequently saw God's body itself lactating, giving birth, clothing our humanness with the spotless humanness of God" (1987, 278). Such a substitution of male for female is a logical consequence of the theological position of sin reflecting the male psychological experience of an intrusive maternal self-object (i.e., defilement) and separation from the same self-object (i.e., abandonment). The substitution occurs in the sacrificial death and resurrection of Christ and is reenacted in the fraction and communion.

3. The Fraction. Once the bread and wine have been consecrated, the celebrant and people say together the Lord's Prayer, in which God the Father is asked to "give us today our daily bread. / Forgive us our sins." The celebrant then breaks apart the bread, in a ritual known as the Fraction. In addition to the practical function of dividing the bread so that each communicant has a piece of the consecrated bread, it has also serves as a symbolic commemoration of the breaking of Christ on the cross. From a self-psychological point of view, the fraction represents the sacrifice of Christ, which in turn symbolizes the fragmentation of the self resulting from the intrusive idealized maternal self-object. The sacrifice becomes the ultimate and final self-fragmentation, which takes away forever the power of the defiling and abandoning maternal self-object and replaces it with a nurturing, masculine holy (undefiled) communion (un-abandonment). This is the self-object function of the sacrificial death of Christ. An argument could be made for Jesus being killed because he advocated the virtues and necessities of a more feminine and maternal (and therefore more powerful and fearful) way of being in the world. In that case the myth of his death as a sacrifice, the establishment of a male apostolic priesthood, and the institution of the eucharist as sacrifice all contradict the very "good news" of Jesus being spread throughout the world.

4. The Distribution of Holy Communion. Following the fragmentation, the celebrant proclaims the words from Paul: "Christ our Passover is sacrificed for us" (1 Cor. 5:7). To which the people reply: "Therefore let us keep the feast" (1 Cor. 5:8). The bread and wine are then distributed to the communicants as the body and blood of Christ, the people being reminded once more that "Christ died for you, and feed on him in your hearts by faith, with thanksgiving." Psychologically, the communicants incorporate the masculine (paternal/filial) self-object function embodied in Christ and symbolized in the bread and wine.

Following the communion, there is a final prayer in which the priest and the people affirm that God has "accepted us as living members of your Son our Savior Jesus Christ, and you have fed us with the spiritual food in the Sacrament of his Body and Blood." After a final blessing, the people are dismissed.

CONCLUSION

PHENOMENOLOGICALLY, SIN AS abandonment or separation requires a sacrifice in order to both expiate the cause of the separation and effect a communion with the ground of social meaning. Sociologically, the male apostolic priests are the gatekeepers who stand between the sinful humanity of which they are a part and the divine that reconciles them and humanity and so ordains them priests. By their act of consecration, fraction, and distribution, communion with the divine is effected. Psychologically, sin represents the intrusion of and abandonment by the idealized maternal imago resulting in narcissistic anxiety. The original psychological experiences of separation, grandiosity, and idealization occur in the narcissistic relation between mother and infant. Males, in turn, are more likely than females to develop a sense of self that is in profound ways fearful, distrustful, envious, and hostile toward women (as Mother).

These three contexts, the phenomenological, sociological, and psychological, have unconsciously fueled the belief that women and their womanliness embody the original cause of abandonment, anxiety, and sin. In order to overcome the sin, a male god who has always existed, thereby eliminating the need for a mother, enters the world through a virgin. The virgin mother is a contradiction that has become one of the cornerstone beliefs of Christianity (based on an Old Testament prophecy). The other cornerstone is the belief that "I [Christ] and the father are one" (John 10:30). This is also a contradiction or at least a psychological impossibility. The theology of the Homoousian doctrine replaces the psychological actuality of "I and the mother are one." Fromm writes that "there is one actual situation in which this [Homoousian] formula makes sense, the situation of the child in the mother's womb" (1955, 67). Fromm neglects the psychological unity between mother and infant maintained by object relations theory and self-psychology, yet his conclusion is still valid: man envies woman and seeks to confiscate her power. As a cultural example of this envy Fromm discusses the Babylonian myth of Thiamat and Marduk. He argues that the myth describes how man first destroys and then recreates with a word rather than a womb. He goes on to claim that the biblical creation story begins where the Babylonian myth ends. "Almost all traces of the supremacy of a female goddess have been eliminated. The creation starts with God's magic, the magic of creation by word" (122). The male psychological foundation of this myth is evident in the theological diminution of women in both the nature of the incarnation and the incarnation's relation to God. Such a theology has a long tradition. But even though Yahweh has been traditionally understood in the Old Testament to be absolutely male, the memory of the "*shekeniah*," the spirit of God, remains a part of popular religious belief. The *shekeniah* is, according to Andrew Greeley, "Yahweh's spouse and the 'Holy Spirit' was imagined, more or less, as a consort of Yahweh" (1972, 152). The place of the Virgin Mary in Roman and Anglican Catholic theology is an example of how the desire for merger with the maternal self-object cannot be eliminated from the psychology of the believer, in spite of the fear of defilement or anger from abandonment.

Conclusion
Toward a Psychoanalytic Theory of Gender and Culture

Men of tormented conscience, or of a criminal imagination, are aware of much that minds of a peaceful, resigned cast do not even suspect. It is not poets alone who dare descend into the abyss of infernal regions, or even who dream of such a descent. The most inexpressive of human beings must have said to himself, at one time or another: "Anything but this!"

Joseph Conrad, *Victory*

There's no initiation either into such mysteries. He has to live in the midst of the incomprehensible, which is also detestable. And it has its fascination, too, that goes to work upon him. The fascination of the abomination—you know, imagine the growing regrets, the longing to escape, the powerless disgust, the surrender, the hate.

Joseph Conrad, *Heart of Darkness*

IN CULTURES THROUGHOUT the world, men have confessed and denied a deep fear and envious resentment toward women. They also harbor an equally profound fascination with them. In this book I have argued that this conscious and not-so-conscious ambivalent anxiety is channeled through and expressed in symbolic ritual blood sacrifice. Its psychological foundations are located in the transitional space between the developing male self and his archaic self-objects, as well as between men and their cultural self-objects in religion and ritual. I outlined the anthropological descriptions of that anxiety in order to probe the psychological questions about sacrifice and male anxiety that anthropology chooses not to answer on its own.

While some compression has been necessary for the sake of economy, the ideas I have pursued in the preceding chapters do suggest a disturbing view of male psychology and religion. I do not claim that the particular interplay of religion, mind, and gender I have presented in these pages is exhaustive. There is of course much more to each of these dimensions. Like a woodcarver I have removed some elements of the matrix, which are part of the reality of culture, in order to bring more clearly into relief the elements of male narcissism and sacrifice. To finish the metaphor, the relief signifies my belief that the view I have given remains grounded in the cultural matrix, into which a return for further understanding and appreciation is quite possible. Any elements left out for the sake of clarity are no less a part of the reality I have represented throughout this book. That reality has remained framed by anthropology but defined by psychoanalytic thought.

I began with a sociological definition of sacrifice as "a religious act which, through the consecration of a victim, modifies the condition of a moral person who accomplishes it or that of certain objects with which he is concerned" (Hubert and Mauss 1964, 13). The social structural basis of a moral condition is the classificatory system of the particular society. Persons, things, and activities are classified and given a moral quality according to the degree to which they resonate with or reverberate back to affective experiences of the classifiers. Both Douglas and Ricoeur argued that the psychological origin of this moral sense (identified as sin and impurity) is related to the dread of defilement. I suggested that the dread of defilement, sin, or intrusion, as well as the dread of abandonment, is the developing self's experience of self-objects during both the early narcissistic period and later reactivation of narcissistic activities, for example, during periods of such classificatory transitions as rites of passage. Victor Turner's analysis of the ritual process focused particularly on liminality as the central concept in rites of passage. Liminality, as anti-structuring communitas, relates not only to the particular transitional and symbolic period (i.e., initiation, sacrifice, death), but to the narcissism that fuels much of the psychic activity within liminal rituals. This seemed particularly evident in Geertz's highly nuanced analysis of Balinese cockfights and male narcissism.

In addition to Geertz's account, I explored the more fully contexualized examples of that narcissistic anxiety embodied in the Malekulan pig sacrifices and the Christian (Episcopal) eucharist. From an academic point of view, these examples might be interesting at best. After all, Malekula no longer exists in the form Layard described, and a late twentieth-century Christian ritual carries little apparent overt influence within the culture where it is practiced. So male narcissism and its relation to women and sacrificial religion may not seem like a very significant topic. If that were the case, this book certainly should never have been written. The significance of male narcissism and women, however, is that while its outward expression in religion and culture may change, the narcissism that fueled the need for the bloody rituals in the first place still remains. Because the narcissistic elements of ritual blood sacrifice exist in the transitional zone of archaic and cultural self-objects, a change in cultural symbols does not necessarily equate with a loss of the psychological basis for these self-object functions altogether. Archaic and untransformed cultural self-objects seek to preserve the idealized and omnipotent experience of narcissism. I suggest that the history of gender relations indicates continuing disturbances in the transmutations of male maternal self-objects.

Male anxiety about women exists today just as it existed in Malekula, just as it has probably existed since men differentiated from women and realized that they were not and could not be the same as the women from whom they came. In both American and Malekulan societies, this narcissistic anxiety is reflected in and fuels subtle and not-so-subtle male violence against women. Most violence against women—assault, incest, rape, and murder—is perpetrated by men who know their victims. And most women who are in prison for violent crimes are there for assaulting or murdering men who abused or otherwise violated them. Men have images, fantasies, or other representations of women that help motivate the violence. In the analytic contract such representational activity is not acted out but rather forms much of the material to be worked through in the transferences. Archaic cultural images of women as objects to be controlled, possessed, punished, or otherwise degraded significantly influence popular or mass culture. Freud was correct when he recognized a connection between the fantasy to degrade a woman and the mother. Freud thought men degrade women in their fantasies because to love them recalls the love of their mothers and activates oedipal incest anxiety. But, as Robert Stolorow and George Atwood (1979) point out, Freud overidealized the oedipal relationship between a son and his mother, and in doing so denied a much deeper ambivalence. If that ambivalence were less repressed, the original object of such feelings of punishment and degradation, now transferred onto other women, might be clarified.

Male narcissism is constantly in need of being recognized, not only by the women who feel its effects, but by men who in the latter days of this century are reluctantly faced with the necessity of changing the way they relate to women and the world. This necessity requires the restructuring of the male self via self-objects that do not function at the expense of women. Winnicott was only half right when he wrote that the future continuation of democracy depends on society not oppressing the mothers who are raising the next generation, no small task indeed. The other half of the restructuring process depends on the emotional availability of paternal self-objects. In Kohut's account of the analysis of Mr. X., the male narcissistic anxiety about women and the necessity of male self-object functions performed by a father are evident:

> It was the task of the analysis to move this need for a firm self—particularly for the pole of the self that was able to carry his idealized goal—from its addictive-erotic representation, which provided only a temporary sense of strength, back to the underlying need to reactivate the relation with the idealized selfobject. Mr. X., in other words, had to reactivate the real relation with the real father of his childhood; he had to shed the Christ-identification his mother had fostered in him, and simultaneously he had to disengage himself from the father-surrogate (the Father of the Trinity—the mother's unconscious imago of her own father) offered him by his mother. It was with the aid of the analytic work focused on the sector of his personality that harbored the need to complete the internalization of the idealized father imago and to integrate the paternal ideal, after the analysis had shifted away from the preoccupation with Mr. X.'s overt grandiosity, that structures began to be built, that a firming of the formerly isolated, unconscious self could take place through gradual transmuting internalization. (1977, 218)

The idealized self-object needed by male humans to continue the development of the self comes from their experience with their fathers, not only with their mothers. If fathers, particularly but not exclusively Western fathers, are not optimally available to their sons during the initial formation of the self, then what is available to internalize may be insufficient to transmute the narcissistic self-objects of infancy and childhood.

The point I am making is that the decline in patriarchal religion has not meant the decline in what Karl Menninger calls a "male narcissism [which] rejects the thesis that woman is biologically and psychologically more important than man" (1942, 41). As noted in previous chapters, women are resented as a gender as much in Malekula as in Christianity and the cultural system replacing it, including that of psychology itself. While Kohut has correctly understood the significance of the role of the self-object in the development of the male self, at times he seems unaware of the sociological significance of what father is available. In American society the father is not only absent or ineffectual (emotionally vague) during the crucial narcissistic periods of male development, but the father who is available also carries with him his own internalized maternal self-object experience and its concomitant narcissistic anxiety. Thus, the "internalization of the idealized father imago" suggested by Kohut would also include the internalization of the narcissistically wounding (intruding and/or abandoning) maternal self-object, regardless of the culture. From the point of view of a theory of culture, I imagine this process as an idealized self-object existing as a male psychic artifact and being passed on from one generation to the next through identification and internalization: a sort of trans-generational mother imago that is never de-idealized, never fully mourned, and never let go. Instead, it is confused with *real* women, and *real* women remain the objects of male narcissistic rage—rage based on the *imago* of women.

Gender and narcissism are central to the development of a self-psychological theory of culture. Although they have recognized the significance of the maternal configuration in the development of psychological structure, self-psychologists are only beginning to discover how men's narcissism differs from women's, and how that narcissism influences and is influenced by the larger, patriarchal culture.

In contemporary society women still give birth to sons and nurture them during the early periods of self-formation. The attitudes of the mother influence the male experience of the maternal self-object. This influence is significant in its depth and consequence. Sometimes the influence is pathological. For example, in a study of three male children who had "threatened or attempted to mutilate their genitals, [and had] . . . expressed an intense wish to be a girl," the children's mothers "suffered from defective object relationships, experienced a sense of emptiness and rage, and were jealous of men" (Lothstein 1988, 215, 227). The relationship between the mother and child led to the creation of an idealized self-object that conveyed "the notion that masculinity was dangerous and dreadful" (227). While recognizing the significance of the self-object in the formation of the self (the gender-self representation), Lothstein cannot place this knowledge within a larger theory of culture. Women are, consciously and/or unconsciously, pained and angered by the conditions men have created for men and women to live in. That attitude could and, in the above cases, does affect the narcissistic development of the male self. In turn the male self reduplicates the social attitudes and structures, which reflect the underlying fear of women experienced by men. It is probably correct to suspect that the little boys Lothstein studied may one day turn their self-destructive idealizations onto female self-objects for what U.S. soldiers in Vietnam called "payback time." Such narcissistic rage leads to the continued devaluation and denigration of women (*see* French 1985, 87–112). The continued devaluation of women leads to a new cycle of women's pain and anger, and so on, and so on.

Because of its emphasis on both social (object) relations and narcissism in the development of the self, self-psychology provides an important addition to the development of a social scientific theory of culture, one that provides the transitional space between the mind (the self) and culture. This book has been an effort to understand the psychology of male narcissism and its relationship to women and culture. A theory of culture that avoids these gender issues has not differentiated enough out of the cultural matrix and is perhaps avoiding, or even unconsciously perpetuating, the very dread embodied in the ritual life of cultures. The faulty idealization of women by men is at the core of much of the world's religions and cultures. The central psychological process in the development of the self is that of the transmuting internalization of de-idealized self-objects, what Peter Homans (1989) calls mourning. The religious and psychological issues I have been discussing in this book reflect the faulty internalization of idealizations. This misguided idealization has been and continues to be the source of great suffering, not just for women, but for all other marginal peoples and creatures of this planet who remain the objects of male narcissistic exploitation. Until men allow themselves to mourn as a significant part of being men, and identify what it is they are mourning, there is little chance that narcissistic violence against women will change.

Yet narcissism is not simply a form of psychopathology. It is the energy and pre-structure of all that is most human about us. Kohut's theory of narcissism also allows us to understand something more deeply about who we are. Introspective self-consciousness and empathic other-awareness—the mature products of narcissism—are the psychological structures that allow us the creativity, humor, wisdom, and empathy to experience the sacredness of reality without being compelled by the injury of some idealized self-object—manifested as narcissistic hunger and rage—to kill, rape, or mutilate that reality. True empathy also forces us not to *ignore* such violations. On the other hand, when the infantile products of narcissism remain the dominant and dominating expressions of a culture, sacred destruction and its secular forms continue to enthrall all but a few disenchanted ones who struggle to de-idealize, who attempt to live beyond the violent symbolizations of these narcissistic creations. I hesitate even to suggest that there are such exceptions for fear that male narcissism will try to hide behind them, allowing men to believe they harbor no such narcissistic resentment toward women. Without being able to recognize such narcissistic resentment, men will continue to extract their "payback" from the idealized surrogate self-objects who gave birth to them. The transformation of faulty idealizations is the key to our survival as a race and planet. Kohut believed that recognizing and changing such perverse idealizations would happen, even though it could take many generations. Before it is too late and men destroy the planet, he hoped there was "enough survival needs in humans that they will suddenly become reasonable" (1985, 226). Then the analyst in him wondered if he was being too optimistic about such transformation (226). It is not simply a matter of being too optimistic or pessimistic about the possibility of becoming reasonable, however, but of first being immersed in the destructive element. Of course, as Conrad warns, "you [and I] may be too much of a fool to go wrong—too dull even to know that you are being assaulted by the powers of darkness" (1947, 560). Yet, I would be grossly wrong if I were to leave you with the impression that by enlightening our dark side, we could eliminate our desires, fears, hatred, or anger toward women. Before enlightenment—if enlightenment is of any lasting value—the darkness needs to be claimed. And claimed not as some disgusting freak of nature *or* culture, to be named and then trotted off and hidden in the nursery closet, but as men's universal inheritance and legacy, indeed as the source of masculine creativity and joy. Conrad remarks that "in every, even terrestrial, mystery there is as it were a sacred core. . . . A universal experience is exactly the sort of thing which is most difficult to appraise justly in a particular instance" (723). Even in the darkness there is a light—in fact, the light of men is in their darkness.

A final note on women. I may have left the impression that women are the hapless victims of men's narcissistic rage, that "being a women is a terribly difficult trade, since it consists principally of dealing with men" (723). That has not been my intention. I have simply left the task of determining the nature and role of women to women. I have a hard enough time figuring out who I am; I would rather struggle with who women tell me they are than tell them who I think they are. "A woman may be a fool, a sleepy fool, an agitated fool, a too awfully noxious fool, and she may even be simply stupid. But she is never dense. She's never made of wood through and through as some men are. There is in woman always, somewhere a spring. Whatever men don't know about women (and it may be a lot, or it may be very little), men and even fathers do know that much. And that is why so many men are afraid of them" (723–24).

Since my life and work have tended to focus on the dark side of life, men have always seemed a little mad to me. Our madness is our grief. I have tried to name—sometimes harshly, sometimes sadly—the essence of that grief. In attempting to recognize the disappointing idealizations for which we long and for which so much of civilization acts as a mirror, I hope I have not been disloyal to men. Our grief is as misty as it is powerful. I would like to think that my conclusion has not been one of reckless contempt for who we are or for what we grieve.

It is when we try to grapple with another man's infinite need that we perceive how incomprehensible, wavering, and misty are the beings that share with us the sight of the stars and the warmth of the sun. It is as if loneliness were a hard and absolute condition of existence; the envelop of flesh and blood on which our eyes are fixed melts before the outstretched hand, and there remains only the capricious, unconsolable, and elusive spirit that no eye can follow, no hand can grasp.

Joseph Conrad, *Lord Jim*

REFERENCES

Allen, M., ed. 1981. *Vanuatu: Politics, Economics and Ritual in Island Melanesia.* Sidney and New York: Academic Press.

Bakan, D. 1966. *The Duality of Human Existence: Isolation and Communion in Western Man.* Boston: Beacon Press.

————. 1968. *Disease, Pain, and Sacrifice: Toward a Psychology of Suffering.* Boston: Beacon Press.

Barrett, S. 1984. *The Rebirth of Anthropological Theory.* Toronto: University of Toronto Press.

Baum, G. 1975. *Religion and Alienation: A Theological Reading of Sociology.* New York: Paulist Press.

Beers, W. 1988. "The *Confessions* of Augustine: Narcissistic Elements." *American Imago* 45:107–25.

Berger, P., and T. Luckmann. 1967. *The Social Construction of Reality: A Treatise in the Sociology of Knowledge.* Garden City, NY: Anchor Books.

Bettelheim, B. 1955. *Symbolic Wounds: Puberty Rites and the Envious Male.* Glencoe, IL: Free Press.

The Book of Common Prayer and Administration of the Sacraments and Other Rites and Ceremonies of the Church According to the Use of the Episcopal Church. 1977. New York: Church Hymnal Corporation and Seabury Press.

Brown, N. 1959. *Life Against Death: The Psychoanalytic Meaning of History.* Middletown, CT: Wesleyan University Press.

Burkert, W. 1972. *Homo Necans: Interpretationen Altergriechischer Operriten und Mythen.* Berlin: Walter de Gruyter.

Bynum, C. 1982. *Jesus as Mother: Studies in the Spirituality of the High Middle Ages.* Berkeley and Los Angeles: University of California Press.

————. 1987. *Holy Feast and Holy Fast: The Religious Significance of Food to Medieval Women.* Berkeley and Los Angeles: University of California Press.

Chodorow, N. 1974. "Family Structure and Feminine Personality." In *Women, Culture and Society,* edited by Michelle Zimbalist Rosaldo and Louise Lamphere, 43–66. Stanford: Stanford University Press.

189

Chowning, A. 1987. "'Women Are Our Business': Women, Exchange and Prestige in Kove." In *Dealing With Inequality: Analyzing Gender Relations in Melanesia and Beyond*, edited by Marilyn Strathern, 130–49. Cambridge and New York: Cambridge University Press.

Comaroff, J. 1985. *Body of Power, Spirit of Resistance: The Culture and History of a South African People*. Chicago: University of Chicago Press.

Conrad, J. 1947. *The Portable Conrad*. Edited by Morton Zabel. New York: Viking Press.

Counts, D. 1990. Introduction. Special Issue: Domestic Violence in Oceania. *Pacific Studies* 13 (3): 1–5.

Cullmann, O. 1953. *Early Christian Worship*. Translated by A. Stewart and James Torrance. Studies in Biblical Theology 10. Chicago: Henry Regnery.

Daly, M. 1973. *Beyond God the Father: Toward a Philosophy of Women's Liberation*. Boston: Beacon Press.

D'Andrade, R. 1958. "Sex Difference and Cultural Institutions." In *Readings in Social Psychology*, edited by Eleanor E. Maccoby, Theodore M. Mewcomb, and Eugene L. Hartley, 180–204. New York: Holt Rinehart and Winston.

Deacon, A. 1934. *Malekula: A Vanishing People in the New Hebrides*. Edited by Camilla H. Wedgwood. London: George Routledge and Sons.

de Heusch, L. 1985. *Sacrifice in Africa: A Structuralist Approach*. Bloomington: Indiana University Press.

De Vos, G., and M. Suarez-Orozco. 1987. "Sacrifice and the Experience of Power." *Journal of Psychoanalytic Anthropology* 10:309–340).

Dilthey, W. 1976. *Selected Writings*. Edited by H. P. Rickman. Cambridge: Cambridge University Press.

Douglas, M. 1966. *Purity and Danger: An Analysis of Pollution and Taboo*. New York: Frederick A. Praeger.

———. 1975. *Implicit Meanings: Essays in Anthropology*. London: Routledge and Kegan Paul.

Ducey, C. 1976. "The Life History and Creative Psychopathology of the Shaman." In *The Psychoanalytic Study of Society*, edited by W. Muensterberger, 7:173–230. New Haven: Yale University Press.

Ducey, M. 1977. *Sunday Morning: Aspects of Urban Ritual*. New York: Free Press.

Durkheim, E. 1915. *The Elementary Forms of the Religious Life*. Translated by Joseph Swain. New York: Free Press.

———. 1938. *The Rules of Sociological Method*. Chicago: University of Chicago Press.

———. 1951. *Suicide*. New York: Free Press.

———. 1964. *The Division of Labor in Society*. New York: Free Press.

Durkheim, E., and M. Mauss. 1963. *Primitive Classification*. Translated and edited by Rodney Needham. Chicago: University of Chicago Press.

Erikson, E. 1968. *Identity, Youth and Crisis*. New York: W. W. Norton.

Evans-Pritchard, E. 1940. *The Nuer: A Description of the Modes of Livelihood and Political Institutions of a Nilotic People*. Oxford: Oxford University Press.

Ferenczi, S. 1956. *Sex and Psycho-Analysis*. London: Dover.

Frazer, J. 1910. *Totemism and Exogamy*. 4 vols. London: Macmillan.

———. 1922. *The Golden Bough: A Study in Magic and Religion*. Abridged ed. New York: Macmillan.

French, M. 1985. *Beyond Power: On Men, Women, and Morals*. New York: Summit Books.

Freud, A. 1973. *The Ego and the Mechanisms of Defense*. New York: International Universities Press.

Freud, S. 1911. "Formations on the Two Principles of Mental Functions." *Standard Edition* 12:213–26. London: Hogarth Press, 1958.

———. 1913. *Totem and Taboo*. *Standard Edition* 13:1–162. London: Hogarth Press, 1955.

———. 1914. "On Narcissism: An Introduction." *Standard Edition* 14:73–102. London: Hogarth Press, 1957.

———. 1915a. "Instincts and Their Vicissitudes." *Standard Edition* 14:117-40. London: Hogarth Press, 1957.

———. 1915b. "The Unconscious." *Standard Edition* 14:166–204. London: Hogarth Press, 1957.

———. 1916–17. *Introductory Lectures on Psychoanalysis*. *Standard Edition* 15–16. London: Hogarth Press, 1963.

———. 1917. "Mourning and Melancholia." *Standard Edition* 14:243–60. London: Hogarth Press, 1957.

———. 1918. "Three Contributions to the Psychology of Love: The Taboo of Virginity." *Standard Edition* 11:163–208. London: Hogarth Press, 1957.

———. 1919a. "A Child in Being Beaten." *Standard Edition* 17:175–204. London: Hogarth Press, 1955.

———. 1919b. "The Uncanny." *Standard Edition* 17:217–56. London: Hogarth Press, 1955.

———. 1920. *Beyond the Pleasure Principle*. *Standard Edition* 18:3–66. London: Hogarth Press, 1955.

———. 1921. *Group Psychology and the Analysis of the Ego*. *Standard Edition* 18:67–144. London: Hogarth Press, 1955.

———. 1923. "The Ego and the Id." *Standard Edition* 19:3–66. London: Hogarth Press, 1961.

———. 1926. "Inhibitions, Symptoms and Anxiety." *Standard Edition* 20:77-172. London: Hogarth Press, 1959.

———. 1931. "Female Sexuality." *Standard Edition* 21:225–43. London: Hogarth Press, 1961.

———. 1933. *New Introductory Lectures on Psychoanalysis Standard Edition* 22:5–182. London: Hogarth Press, 1964.

———. 1940. "An Outline of Psychoanalysis." *Standard Edition* 23:144–207. London: Hogarth Press, 1964.

Fromm, E. 1955. *The Dogma of Christ and Other Essays on Religion, Psychology and Culture*. New York: Holt, Rinehart and Winston.

Funabiki, T. 1981. "On Pigs of the Mbotgote in Malekula." In *Vanuatu: Politics, Economics and Ritual in Island Melanesia*, edited by Michael Allen, 173–88. Sidney and New York: Academic Press.

Geertz, C. 1973. *The Interpretation of Cultures*. New York: Basic Books.

Gelber, M. 1986. *Gender and Society in the New Guinea Highlands: An Anthropological Perspective on Antagonism Toward Women*. Boulder and London: Westview Press.

Girard, R. 1977. *Violence and the Sacred*. Translated by Patrick Gregory. Baltimore: Johns Hopkins University Press.

Goldberg, A., ed. 1978. *The Psychology of the Self: A Case Book*. New York: International Universities Press.

Greeley, A. 1972. *Religion: A Secular Theory*. New York: Free Press.

Harrison, T. 1939. *Savage Civilization*. London: Victor Gollancy.

Hartmann, H., and R. Lowenstein. 1964. "Comments on the Formation of Psychic Structure." In *Papers on Psychoanalytic Psychology* 14. Psychological Issues Series, edited by Heinz Hartmann, Ernst Kris, and R. M. Lowenstein, 27–55. New York: International Universities Press.

Herdt, G. 1981a. *Guardians of the Flute: Idioms of Masculinity*. New York: McGraw-Hill.

——. 1981b. *The Sambia: Ritual and Gender in New Guinea*. New York: Holt, Rinehart and Winston.

——, ed. 1982. *Rituals of Manhood: Male Initiation in Papua New Guinea*. Berkeley and Los Angeles: University of California Press.

Herdt, G. and M. Stephen. 1989. *The Religious Imagination in New Guinea*. New Brunswick, NJ: Rutgers University Press.

Homans, P. 1979. *Jung in Context: Modernity and the Making of a Psychology*. Chicago: University of Chicago Press.

——. 1984. "Once Again, Psychoanalysis East and West: A Psychoanalytic Essay on Religion, Mourning, and Healing." *History of Religions* 24:133–54.

——. 1989. *The Ability to Mourn: Disillusionment and the Social Origins of Psychoanalysis*. Chicago: University of Chicago Press.

Hubert, H., and M. Mauss. 1964. *Sacrifice: Its Nature and Function*. Translated by W. D. Halls. Chicago: University of Chicago Press.

James, M. 1973. "Review of *The Analysis of the Self* by Heinz Kohut." *International Journal of Psycho-Analysis* 52:363–68.

James, W. 1958. *The Varieties of Religious Experience: A Study in Human Nature*. New York: Mentor Book.

Jay, N. 1985. "Sacrifice as Remedy for Having Been Born of Woman." In *Immaculate and Powerful: The Female in Sacred Image and Social Reality*, edited by Clarissa W. Atkinson, Constance H. Buchanan, and Margaret R. Miles, 283–309. Boston: Beacon Press.

Jolly, M. 1981. "People and Their Products in South Pentecost." In *Vanuatu: Politics, Economics and Ritual in Island Melanesia*, edited by Michael Allen, 269–94. Sidney and New York: Academic Press.

Jung, C. 1939. *The Integration of the Personality*. Translated by S. M. Dell. New York: Farrar and Rinehart.

——. 1959. *The Archetypes of the Collective Unconscious. Collected Works* 9, pt. 1. Princeton: Princeton University Press.

——. 1967. *Symbols of Transformation: An Analysis of the Prelude to a Case of Schizophrenia. Collected Works* 5. Princeton: Princeton University Press.

Kakar, S. 1982. *Shamans, Mystics and Doctors: A Psychological Inquiry into India and Its Healing Tradition*. Boston: Beacon Press.

Kernberg, O. 1975. *Borderline Conditions and Pathological Narcissism*. New York: Jason Aronson.

Kessing, R. 1982. *Kwaio Religion: The Living and the Dead in a Solomon Island*. New York: Columbia University Press.

——. 1987. "Ta'a geni: Women's Perspectives on Kwaio Society." In *Dealing with Inequality: Analyzing Gender Relations in Melanesia and Beyond*, edited by Marilyn Strathern, 33–62. Cambridge and New York: Cambridge University Press.

Khan, M. 1981. "From Masochism to Psychic Pain." *International Journal of Psychoanalysis* 60:413–23.

Kierkegaard, S. 1946. *The Concept of Dread*. Translated by Walter Lowrie. Princeton: Princeton University Press.

Klein, M. 1963. *Our Adult World and Other Essays*. London: Heineman Medical Books.

——. 1986. *The Selected Klein*. Edited by Juliet Mitchell. New York: Free Press.

Kohut, H. 1971. *The Analysis of the Self: A Systematic Approach to the Psychoanalytic Treatment of Narcissistic Personality Disorders*. New York: International Universities Press.

——. 1977. *The Restoration of the Self*. Madison, CT: International Universities Press.

——. 1978. *The Search for the Self: Selected Writings of Heinz Kohut: 1950–1978*. 2 vols. Edited by Paul Ornstein. New York: International Universities Press.

——. 1984. *How Does Analysis Cure?* Chicago: University of Chicago Press.

——. 1985. *Self Psychology and the Humanities: Reflections on a New Psychoanalytic Approach*. Edited by Charles Strozier. New York: W. W. Norton.

Lawrence, P., and M. Meggitt, eds. 1965. *Gods, Ghosts and Men in Melanesia: Some Religions of Australian New Guinea and the New Hebrides*. Melbourne, Australia: Oxford University Press.

Layard, J. 1942. *Stone Men of Malekula: Vao*. London: Chatto and Windus.

Lévi-Strauss, C. 1963. *Totemism*. Translated by Rodney Needham. Boston: Beacon Press.

——. 1964. *Tristes Tropiques*. Translated by John Russell. New York: Atheneum.

——. 1966. *The Savage Mind*. London: Weidenfeld and Nicholson.

——. 1967. *Structural Anthropology*. Translated by Claire Jacobson and Brooke Grundfest Schoepf. Garden City, NY: Anchor Books

———. 1969. *Elementary Structures of Kinship*. Translated by James Bell and John Richard von Strurmer. Boston: Beacon Press.

———. 1978. *Myth and Meaning*. Toronto: University of Toronto Press.

Lidz, T., and R. Lidz. 1989. *Oedipus in the Stone Age: A Psychoanalytic Study of Masculinization in Papua New Guinea*. Madison, CT: International Universities Press.

Lienhardt, G. 1961. *Divinity and Experience: The Religion of the Dinka*. Oxford: Clarendon Press.

Lifton, R. 1976. *The Life of the Self: Toward a New Psychology*. New York: Simon and Schuster.

Longfellow, H. n.d. "The Song of Hiawatha." In *The Poems of Henry Wadsworth Longfellow*. New York: Modern Library.

Lothstein, L. 1988. "Selfobject Failure and Gender Identity." In *Frontiers in Self Psychology*, edited by Arnold Goldberg, 3:213–35. Hillsdale, NJ: Analytic Press.

MacCormack, C. 1980. "Nature, Culture and Gender: A Critique." In *Nature, Culture and Gender*, edited by Carol P. MacCormack and Marilyn Strathern, 1–24. Cambridge: Cambridge University Press.

McGuire, M. 1981. *Religion: The Social Context*. Belmont, CA: Wadsworth.

Mahler, M. 1968. *On Human Symbiosis and the Vicissitudes of Individuation*. New York: International Universities Press.

Mahler, M., F. Pine, and A. Bergman. 1975. *The Psychological Birth of the Infant*. New York: Basic Books.

Mann, T. 1936. *Death in Venice*. In *Stories of Three Decades*. Translated by H. T. Lowe-Porter. New York: Alfred A. Knopf.

Mauss, M. 1954. *The Gift*. Translated by I. Cunnison. London: Cohen and West.

May, H., and B. Metzger, eds. 1965. *The Oxford Annotated Bible with the Apocrypha*. RSV. New York: Oxford University Press.

Meigs, A. 1984. *Food, Sex, and Pollution: A New Guinea Religion*. New Brunswick, NJ: Rutgers University Press.

Menninger, K. 1942. *Love Against Hate*. New York: Harcourt, Brace.

Milner, M. 1955. "The Role of Illusion in Symbol Formation." In *New Directions in Psychoanalysis: The Significance of Infant Conflict in the Pattern of Adult Behavior*, edited by Melanie Klein, Paula Heiman, and R. E. Money-Kyrle, 82–108. London: Tavistock Publications.

Mitchell, J. 1974. *Psychoanalysis and Feminism*. New York: Pantheon Books.

Money-Kyrle, R. 1930. *The Meaning of Sacrifice*. London: Hogarth Press.

Nandy, A. 1976. "Woman Versus Womanliness." *Psychoanalytic Review* 63:301–15.

Neumann, E. 1963. *The Great Mother: An Analysis of an Archetype*. Translated by Ralph Manheim. Princeton: Princeton University Press.

———. 1973. *The Child: Structure and Dynamics of the Nascent Personality*. New York: G. P. Putnam's Sons.

Obeyesekere, G. 1990. *The Work of Culture: Symbolic Transformation in Psychoanalysis and Anthropology*. Chicago: University of Chicago Press.

Patterson, M. 1981. "Slings and Arrows: Rituals of Status Acquisition on North Ambrym." In *Vanuatu: Politics, Economics and Ritual in Island Melanesia*, edited by Michael Allen, 189–236. Sidney and New York: Academic Press.

Philipson, I. 1985. "Gender and Narcissism." *Psychology of Women Quarterly* 9:213–28.

Piaget, J. 1968. *Structuralism*. Translated by Chaninah Maschler. New York: Harper Torchbooks.

Progoff, I. 1973. *Jung's Psychology and Its Social Meaning*. Garden City, NY: Anchor Books.

Reik, T. 1930. *Ritual: Psychoanalytic Studies*. Translated by D. Byran. London: Hogarth Press.

———. 1957. *Myth and Guilt: The Crime and Punishment of Mankind*. New York: George Braziller.

Ricoeur, P. 1967. *The Symbolism of Evil*. Translated by Emerson Buchanan. New York: Harper and Row.

———. 1970. *Freud and Philosophy: An Essay on Interpretation*. Translated by Denis Savage. New Haven: Yale University Press.

Robinson, T. 1920. "Genesis." In *The Abingdon Bible Commentary*, edited by Frederick Eiselen, Edwin Lewis, and David Downey, 217–48. New York: Abingdon-Cokebury Press.

Rosaldo, M., and L. Lamphere, eds. 1974. *Women, Culture and Society*. Stanford, CA: Stanford University Press.

Ross, M., and C. Ross. 1983. "Mothers, Infants, and the Psychoanalytic Study of Ritual." *Signs: Journal of Women in Culture and Society* 9:26–39.

Ruether, R., and R. Keller. 1981. *Women and Religion*. Vol. 4, *1900–1968*. San Francisco: Harper and Row.

Sagan, E. 1974. *Cannibalism: Human Aggression and Cultural Form*. New York: Harper and Row.

———. 1979. *The Lust to Annihilate: A Psychoanalytic Study of Violence in Ancient Greek Culture*. New York: Psychohistory Press.

———. 1985. *At the Dawn of Tyranny: The Origins of Individuality, Political Oppression, and the State*. New York: Alfred A. Knopf.

Smith, W. Robertson. 1894. *Lectures on the Religion of the Semites*, 2d. ed. London: A. and C. Black.

Stein, M. 1976. "Narcissus." *Spring* 1976:32–53.

Stevens, A. 1982. *Archetypes: A Natural History of the Self*. New York: Quill.

Stolorow, R., and G. Atwood. 1979. *Faces in a Cloud: Subjectivity in Personality Theory*. New York: Jason Aronson.

Strathern, M., ed. 1987. *Dealing with Inequality: Analyzing Gender Relations in Melanesia and Beyond*. Cambridge: Cambridge University Press.

———. 1988. *The Gender of the Gift: Problems with Women and Problems with Society in Melanesia*. Berkeley and Los Angeles: University of California Press.

Tiger, L. 1969. *Men in Groups*. London: Thomas Nelson and Sons.

Turner, V. 1964. "Betwixt and Between: The Liminal Period in *Rites of Passage*." In *Proceedings of the American Ethnological Society for 1964*, 4–20. Seattle: University of Washington Press.

———. 1967. *Forest of Symbols: Aspects of Ndembu Ritual*. Ithaca, NY: Cornell University Press.

———. 1969. *The Ritual Process: Structure and Anti-Structure*. Chicago: Aldine.

———. 1977. "Sacrifice as Quintessential Process: Prophylaxis or Abandonment?" *History of Religions* 16:189–215.

———. 1978. "Encounter With Freud: The Making of a Comparative Symbologist." In *The Making of Psychological Anthropology*, edited by George D. Spindler, 558–83. Berkeley and Los Angeles: University of California Press.

———. 1985. *On the Edge of the Bush: Anthropology as Experience*. Edited by Edith Turner. Tucson: University of Arizona Press.

Turner, V., and E. Bruner, eds. 1986. *The Anthropology of Experience*. Urbana: University of Illinois Press.

Turner, V., and E. Turner. 1978. *Image and Pilgrimage in Christian Culture: Anthropological Perspectives*. New York: Columbia University Press.

Tylor, E. 1871. *Primitive Culture: Researches into the Development of Mythology, Philosophy, Religion, Art and Custom*, 2 vols. London: J. Murray.

———. 1878. *Researches into the Early History of Mankind and the Development of Civilization*. Boston: Estes and Lauriate.

van der Leuuw, G. 1938. *Religion in Essence and Manifestation: A Study in Phenomenology*. Translated by J. E. Turner. London: George Allen and Unwin.

van Gennep, A. 1960. *The Rites of Passage*. Translated by M. Vizedom and G. Caffee. Chicago: University of Chicago Press.

Verdesi, E. 1976. *In But Still Out: Women and the Church*. Philadelphia: Westminster Press.

Weinstein, F., and G. Platt. 1973. *Psychoanalytic Sociology: An Essay on the Interpretation of Historical Data and the Phenomenon of Collective Behavior*. Baltimore: Johns Hopkins University Press.

Whitehead, A. 1927. *Symbolism*. New York: Capricorn Books.

Winnicott, D. 1965a. *The Family and Individual Development*. London: Tavistock.

———. 1965b. *The Maturational Processes and the Facilitating Environment: Studies in the Theory of Emotional Development*. Madison, CT: International Universities Press.

———. 1971a. *Playing and Reality*. New York: Tavistock.

———. 1971b. *Therapeutic Consultations in Child Psychiatry*. New York: Basic Books.

———. 1986. *Home Is Where We Start From: Essays by a Psychoanalyst*. Edited by Claire Winnicott, Ray Shepard, and Madeleine Davis. New York: W. W. Norton.

Young, M. 1987. "The Tusk, the Flute and the Serpent: Disguise and Revelation in Goodenough Mythology." In *Dealing with Inequality: Analyzing Gender Relations in Melanesia and Beyond*, edited by Marilyn Strathern, 33–62. Cambridge: Cambridge University Press.

INDEX

197